CW00826083

Paradise & Hell

By
Shaykh Mufti Saiful Islām

JKN Publications

© Copyright by JKN Publications

First Published in June 2015

ISBN 978-1-909114-08-1

British Library Cataloguing in Publication Data
A catalogue record for this book is available from the British Library.

All Rights Reserved. No part of this book may be reproduced, stored in a retrieval system or transmitted in any form or by any means, electronic, mechanical, photocopying, recording or otherwise, without the prior permission of the copyright owner.

Publisher's Note:

Every care and attention has been put into the production of this book. If however, you find any errors, they are our own, for which we seek Allāh's ﷻ forgiveness and the reader's pardon.

Published by:

JKN Publications
118 Manningham Lane
Bradford
West Yorkshire
BD8 7JF
United Kingdom

t: +44 (0) 1274 308 456 | w: www.jkn.org.uk | e: info@jkn.org.uk

Book Title: Paradise & Hell

Author: Shaykh Mufti Saiful Islām

Printed in Turkey by MEGA Printing

"In the Name of Allāh, the Most Beneficent,
the Most Merciful"

Contents

Introduction

All praises are due to Allāh ﷻ. May peace, salutations and blessings be upon our guide, mentor and beloved Prophet Muhammad ﷺ, upon his noble Sahābahs ؆, Tābieen and upon those who follow their noble lifestyles until the Day of Judgement.

Allāh ﷻ created this world for a limited period of time, full of trials, worries, hardships and troubles. This makes worshipping Allāh ﷻ and fulfilling the obligations set by Him through Islām easier to attain the great favours, bounties and benefits in the ever lasting Hereafter. The Hereafter consists of a reward for humanity, Paradise and a punishment for humanity, Hell.

Jannah (Paradise) is an Arabic word meaning a matter which is concealed and hidden. Jannah is veiled from our selective visions in this world and we are told by our Creator to believe in it without seeing.

By the grace of Allāh ﷻ, my beloved Shaykh, Mufti Saiful Islām Sāhib has authored, collected and compiled this book, 'Paradise & Hell' so that the reader can understand the innumerable favours, reward, comfort and unlimited luxuries of Paradise. Furthermore, the reader can also understand the description and punishments of Hell, its fire, inhabitants, curses and agony etc.. My beloved Shaykh has also used a unique format to make this presentable by including the Tafseer and virtues of Sūrah Ar-Rahmān.

Allāh ﷻ discusses the various favours that He has blessed man and Jinn with. These favours are tremendous and benefit people in this world and in the Hereafter. In the entire Sūrah, Allāh's ﷻ bounties, worldly as well as spiritual are continuously reminded. The greatest of all bounties is the knowledge of the Holy Qur'ān because it is an all-comprehensive Book directing man in worldly and spiritual matters.

As well as the bounties, Allāh ﷻ also mentions in Sūrah Ar-Rahmān the horrific punishments in Hell. Hence the reason as to why my beloved teacher has included this Sūrah in explaining Paradise and Hell.

May Allāh ﷻ bestow His eternal blessings upon all those who assisted in the production of this book namely my beloved teacher and Shaykh, Mufti Saiful Islām Sāhib, for sacrificing their time and effort in making this book presentable to the masses for the sake of pleasing our Creator, Allāh ﷻ and propagating the Deen of Islām. Āmeen!

Maulāna Ismāeel Aziz
Graduate of JKN
June 2015

Virtues of Sūrah Ar-Rahmān

On the authority of Sayyidunā Jābir Ibn Abdullāh ﷺ that the Holy Prophet ﷺ came to his Companions and recited Sūrah Ar-Rahmān from the beginning to the end and they all kept quiet. So he said, "Why do I see you so quiet. I had recited it (Sūrah Ar-Rahmān) to the Jinns and they were more responsive than you are. Whenever I came across the verse, **"So which favours of your Lord do the two of you deny?"** The Jinns would say, "There is nothing among your bounties that we can deny, praise be to You.'" (Tirmizi)

Sayyidunā Ali ﷺ says that he heard the Holy Prophet ﷺ saying, "Everything has its elegance and the elegance of the Holy Qur'ān is Sūrah Ar-Rahmān." (Baihaqi)

Imām Ahmad ﷺ recorded in his Musnad that a man asked Sayyidunā Abdullāh Ibn Mas'ood ﷺ, "How is this recited, Mā'in Ghayri Yāsin or Āsin?" He asked him, "Are you that proficient in reciting the whole Qur'ān?" He replied, "I recited the Mufassal section in one Rak'at." So he said, "Woe to you? Do you recite the Holy Qur'ān in haste as if it is poetry? I know that the Holy Prophet ﷺ used to recite two Sūrahs from the beginning of the Mufassal section in one Rak'at." Sayyidunā Abdullāh Ibn Mas'ood ﷺ considered Sūrah Ar-Rahmān to be at the beginning of the Mufassal section.

In Sūrah Ar-Rahmān, Allāh ﷻ discusses the various favours that He has blessed man and Jinn with. These favours are tremendous and benefit people in this world and in the Hereafter. Allāh ﷻ repeats the verse, **"So which favours of your Lord do the two of you deny?"** thirty one times in the Sūrah. This creates great beauty to the Sūrah in terms of recitation and meaning.

Sūrah Ar-Rahmān was revealed in Makkah. The opening word of the first verse of the Sūrah is Ar-Rahmān. One of the reasons for beginning the Sūrah with this name of Allāh ﷻ is that the polytheists of Makkah were unaware of this name of Allāh ﷻ. They used to say, "What is Ar-Rahmān?" as mentioned in Sūrah Al-Furqān, verse 60. This name has been selected here to inform them who is Ar-Rahmān. The second reason is to indicate that teaching the Holy Qur'ān which has been mentioned in the next verse as Allāh's ﷻ act, is a great gift bestowed through His sheer infinite grace. It is not because this or any other act is obligatory on Allāh ﷻ for which He could be held responsible, nor because He is in need of anyone. He has taught the Holy Qur'ān only through His grace.

In the entire Sūrah, Allāh's ﷻ bounties, worldly as well as spiritual are continuously reminded. The greatest of all bounties is the knowledge of the Holy Qur'ān because it is an all-comprehensive Book directing man in worldly and spiritual matters. Those who acted upon the Holy Qur'ān and fulfilled its right, like the blessed Companions, Allāh ﷻ raised their status in the Hereafter and blessed them with inconceivable and amazing bounties and favours. Even in this world they reached such a status and position that even the greatest kings could not dream of.

Virtues of the Holy Qur'ān

The Holy Qur'ān is an extremely great bounty of Allāh ﷻ to mankind. Allāh ﷻ taught man the words of the Holy Qur'ān and the meanings of the verses. He has also allowed man to understand the eloquence and rhetoric of the Holy Qur'ān. In addition to this, Allāh ﷻ has also made it easy for man to memorise the Holy Qur'ān. Man who is merely an entity filled with waste and blood is extremely honoured to be able to contain the speech of Allāh ﷻ in his bosom and to speak it with his tongue.

Thousands of books have been written containing explanations of the Holy Qur'ān and this practice will continue until the Day of Judgement.

Sayyidunā Uthmān ؓ narrates that the Holy Prophet ﷺ said, "The best among you is he who learns the Holy Qur'ān and teaches it." (Bukhāri)

The Holy Qur'ān is the basis and foundation of Deen and on the preservation and propagation of the Holy Qur'ān depends the very existence of faith. Hence, the virtue of learning and teaching the Holy Qur'ān is self evident and does not need further elucidation. This Hadeeth is further supported by another Hadeeth as reported by Sayyidunā Saeed Ibn Saleem ؓ, "If a person who has acquired knowledge of the Holy Qur'ān considers another person who has been gifted with something else to be more fortunate than himself, then he has shown disrespect to the blessings of Allāh ﷻ bestowed on him on account of his learning the Holy Qur'ān." It is

10

evident that since the Holy Qur'ān is the word of Allāh ﷻ, it is superior to all other discourses.

Sayyidunā Abdullāh Ibn Abbās ؓ reports that the Holy Prophet ﷺ said, "The best of my Ummah are the bearers of the Holy Qur'ān and those who stay awake (in worship) at night." (Mishkāt)

Sayyidunā Abdullāh Ibn Amr ؓ reports that the Holy Prophet ﷺ said, "On the Day of Judgement, it will be said to the person devoted to the Holy Qur'ān, "Go on reciting the Holy Qur'ān and continue ascending the storeys of Paradise and recite in the slow manner you had been reciting in the world. Your final abode will be where you reach at the time of the last verse of your recitation."'

(Abū Dāwood, Tirmizi)

'The person of the Holy Qur'ān' apparently means a Hāfiz. Mulla Ali Qāri ؒ has explained that this honour is reserved for a Hāfiz and that this Hadeeth does not apply to one who recites by looking into the Holy Qur'ān. Firstly, because the words 'a person of the Holy Qur'ān' point towards a Hāfiz and secondly, there is a Hadeeth in Musnad Ahmad which states, "Till he recites of whatever Qur'ān is with him." This word more clearly refers to a Hāfiz, although a reader who remains very often engaged in reciting the Holy Qur'ān may also be implied.

Sayyidunā Mu'āz ؓ reports that the Holy Prophet ﷺ said, "Whoever recites the Holy Qur'ān and acts upon what is contained in it, his parents will be made to wear a crown on the Day of

Judgement, the brilliance of which will excel that of the sun, if the same were within your worldly houses. So what do you think about the person who himself acts upon it?"

(Abū Dāwood, Tirmizi)

Regarding the status of a Hāfiz, it is mentioned in a Hadeeth narrated by Imām Tirmizi 🏵 on the authority of Sayyidunā Ali 🏵 that the Holy Prophet 🏵 said, "Whoever recites the Holy Qur'ān and learns it by heart and embodies what it makes lawful as lawful and its unlawful as forbidden, will be admitted into Paradise by Allāh 🏵 Who will also accept his intercession in respect of ten such individuals of his family who shall have been destined to Hell."

(Ahmad, Tirmizi)

By the grace of Allāh 🏵, entry into Paradise is ensured for every believer though it may come after being punished for his misdeeds. The Hāfiz will however be favoured with this entry right from the beginning. The ten individuals in whose favour his intercession will be accepted will be those sinful and disobedient Muslims who are guilty of major sins. There can be no intercession however, for the disbelievers. Those who are not Hāfiz and cannot memorise the Holy Qur'ān should at least make one of their relatives a Hāfiz so that by His grace, they may be saved from their own evil doings.

Creation of Mankind

بِسۡمِ اللهِ الرَّحۡمٰنِ الرَّحِيۡمِ

In the Name of Allāh, the Merciful, the Beneficent.

الرَّحۡمٰنُ

The Most Merciful.

عَلَّمَ الۡقُرۡآنَ

Taught the Qur'ān.

خَلَقَ الۡإِنۡسَانَ

He created Man.

عَلَّمَهُ الۡبَيَانَ

Taught him to speak.

The opening verses of Sūrah Ar-Rahmān mention the bounties and favours that are connected to Imān, soul and body. As previously mentioned, it is through His sheer mercy that He has enabled us to recite the Holy Qur'ān.

Allāh ﷻ continues, **"He created man and taught him to speak."** Allāh ﷻ granted man knowledge, granted him the ability to speak and even taught him how to utilise this ability. Man can thus, express what he feels and thinks. Allāh ﷻ has also taught man how to speak eloquently and how to explain the meanings of the Holy Qur'ān. Not only did Allāh ﷻ teach people speech, but He taught man various languages and manners of expression.

He says,

وَمِنْ آيَاتِهِ خَلْقُ السَّمَاوَاتِ وَالْأَرْضِ وَاخْتِلَافُ أَلْسِنَتِكُمْ وَأَلْوَانِكُمْ إِنَّ فِي ذَلِكَ لَآيَاتٍ لِلْعَالِمِينَ

"And among His signs is the creation of the heavens and the earth and the difference of your languages and colours. Verily, in that are signs for men of sound knowledge." (30:22)

The wisdom behind mentioning the bounty of Qur'anic knowledge first and the creation of man later is that the fundamental objective of man's creation is to impart to him the knowledge of the Holy Qur'ān and for him to follow its guidance as stated elsewhere in the Holy Qur'ān.

وَمَا خَلَقْتُ الْجِنَّ وَالْإِنْسَ إِلَّا لِيَعْبُدُونِ

"And I did not create the Jinns and the human beings except that they should worship Me." (51:56)

Surely, worship without Divine guidance is not possible. The source of the Divine guidance is the Holy Qur'ān. Thus Qur'anic knowledge is mentioned before man's creation.

Having created man, uncountable bounties are bestowed upon

him. Of them, imparting the knowledge of expression has been mentioned especially because the bounties necessary for man's growth and development and his existence and survival like his food and water, his protection against cold and heat, his residential arrangements and so on, are bounties in which all creatures are equal partners. Among the bounties that are exclusive to human beings, knowledge of the Holy Qur'ān has been mentioned first, followed by the knowledge of expression because deriving benefit from the Holy Qur'ān and imparting it to others is dependent on the knowledge of expression.

The word Bayān (to express oneself) encompasses means of communication created by Allāh ﷻ like speech, writing etc. There are various languages and dialects of various communities of the world. All these are a constituent part of linguistic knowledge which is the practical interpretation or application of the verse,

$$وَعَلَّمَ آدَمَ الْأَسْمَآءَ كُلَّهَا$$

"And He taught Ādam the names (and meanings and qualities of all things)." (2:31)

Sun and the Moon

Verses 5 and 6

$$الشَّمْسُ وَالْقَمَرُ بِحُسْبَانٍ$$

"The sun and moon (orbit in) calculated courses."

15

وَالنَّجْمُ وَالشَّجَرُ يَسْجُدَانِ

"And the creeper and the tree prostrate."

Verse 5 draws attention to the celestial bodies from among the bounties of Allāh ﷻ. They are especially mentioned because the entire system of the world depends on the movement of theses bodies in their orbits in perfect succession, according to precise calculation that is never delayed nor disturbed.

In Sūrah Yāseen, Allāh ﷻ beautifully explains the duty of the sun and the moon.

وَالشَّمْسُ تَجْرِي لِمُسْتَقَرٍّ لَّهَا ذَلِكَ تَقْدِيرُ الْعَزِيزِ الْعَلِيمِ وَالْقَمَرَ قَدَّرْنَاهُ مَنَازِلَ حَتَّى عَادَ كَالْعُرْجُونِ الْقَدِيمِ. لَا الشَّمْسُ يَنْبَغِي لَهَا أَنْ تُدْرِكَ الْقَمَرَ وَلَا اللَّيْلُ سَابِقُ النَّهَارِ وَكُلٌّ فِي فَلَكٍ يَسْبَحُونَ

"And the sun runs on its fixed course for a term (appointed). That is the decree of the All-Mighty, the All-Knowing. And the moon, We have measured for it stations (to traverse) till it returns like the old dried curved date stalk. It is not for the sun to overtake the moon, nor does the night outstrip the day. They all float, each in an orbit." (36:38-40)

The word 'Husbān' with Dhammah on the first letter, according to some grammarians is used in the sense of 'Hisāb', meaning to calculate. Other grammarians feel that Husbān is the plural of Hisāb. The meaning of the verse, according to the former grammarians would be: The two bodies on which depends man's entire life, run on fixed courses. They are subject to certain laws and they perform regularly and punctually their allocated tasks (alternation of night and day, change of seasons and determination of years and months) according to a calculation. If we go by the latter grammarians' interpretation that Husbān is the plural of Hisāb, then it will refer to the fact that the sun and the moon each has its own calculated orbits. The entire solar system is proceeding on the basis of different calculations and each one of them is so firm and accurate that no deviation has ever occurred.

This age is regarded as an age of ascension for science. The marvellous new inventions of the scientific age have caused wonders even for the philosophers. However, there is a clear difference between human inventions and Divine creation, which every intelligent person can observe. Human inventions are subject to a series of continuous breakdowns and damage, which require servicing, repair or refurbishment. A machine, no matter how strong or sophisticated, needs to be repaired or at least serviced after a while. If this is not done in time, it will remain useless. The massive Divine creation, on the other hand needs no repair, no servicing nor refurbishing at any time. Neither the solar system overtakes the lunar movement, nor does the lunar movement outstrip the solar system. The sun and the moon and other celestial bodies float and move in their own orbits.

Creeper and the Tree

In verse 6, **"The creeper and the tree prostrate,"** the word 'Najm' refers to plants having no stem and the word 'Shajar' refers to any

17

tree with stems or trunk, twigs and branches. All of them prostrate to Allāh 🕮. Sajdah is the highest peak of humility, respect, surrender and unconditional love and obedience of Allāh 🕮. In this context, the verse means that Allāh 🕮 has assigned a specific task to every tree, plant, creeper and their leaves and fruits for the benefit of mankind and they are performing their tasks without the slightest deviation from their assigned duties. The plants without stems and the trees humbly submit themselves to Allāh's 🕮 will.

Thus, everything from the largest celestial body to the smallest plant is subject to this law which is manifest in nature.

There are two types of obedience that are carried out. The first is free will, for instance, man and Jinn are given free will to choose between obeying Allāh's 🕮 laws or disobeying them. All other creations of Allāh 🕮 are assigned specific tasks or duties to perform without any choice. The latter is referred to as 'Itā'ah Takweeniyyah' or 'Jabriyyah'- compelled obedience. In this present verse, the word 'Sajdah' refers to this type of obedience to Allāh's 🕮 law in nature, where the natural objects have no choice.

Scales of Allāh 🕮

Verses 7 and 8

وَالسَّمَآءَ رَفَعَهَا وَوَضَعَ الْمِيْزَانَ

"Allāh raised the sky and erected the scale."

أَلَّا تَطْغَوْا فِي الْمِيْزَانِ

"So that you do not transgress in the matters of the scale."

The words used in the verse are 'Rafa'a' and 'Wada'a' which are antonyms; Rafa'a means to raise whereas, Wada'a means to put down. The first verse describes that Allāh ﷻ has raised the heavens. This can imply both literal and metaphorical interpretation; if it is literal, then it implies raising the sky in its physical height and if it is metaphorical, then it would refer to the high status of the heaven. In relation to the earth, the heaven occupies a higher position. Normally, the earth is understood to be the opposite of heaven, so from this perspective, they are both mentioned throughout the Holy Qur'ān as opposite to one another.

After mentioning the high position of the heavens, the Holy Qur'ān further explains that Allāh ﷻ has erected the scale. In the verse, the word 'Meezān' has been interpreted as scale. Scholars such as Mujāhid ﷺ, Qatādah ﷺ, Suddi ﷺ and others, interpret it as justice because that is the prime objective of the existence of the Meezān (scale). Some scholars have explained it in the apparent sense that it is an equipment used to determine the weight of mankind's deeds as well as other things. This equipment could be a scale consisting of a bar with a pan or a dish at each end or could be similar to a modern equipment used for the purpose of measuring and weighing. As a result, from this interpretation it would mean to maintain the rights (of others) and establish justice and fair play in dealings.

19

In verse 7, Allāh ﷻ mentions the creation of the scale and explains the reason for its creation in the following verse (verse 8). The verb تطغو (Tatghaw) is derived from the word طغيان (Tughyān) which means to commit injustice. So both verses would imply that the Meezān or scale has been created so that you do not transgress the limits set by Allāh ﷻ and do not commit any injustice against others.

$$\text{وَأَقِيمُوا الْوَزْنَ بِالْقِسْطِ وَلَا تُخْسِرُوا الْمِيزَانَ}$$

"And so that you establish the scale with justice and you do not make the scale deficient."

Allāh ﷻ begins the verse positively and then, concludes it in the negative. So both aspects of the injunction would mean; So maintain justice and fairness and do not deceive in weighing and measuring. Allāh ﷻ is warning mankind not to demand anything extra in weighing once dues are given to him and neither, to reduce the weight when payment is due upon him.

Justice in Weighing

This evil practice has been explained in the opening verses of Sūrah Al-Mutaffifeen,

$$\text{وَيْلٌ لِّلْمُطَفِّفِينَ . الَّذِينَ إِذَا اكْتَالُوا عَلَى النَّاسِ يَسْتَوْفُونَ . وَإِذَا كَالُوهُمْ أَو وَّزَنُوهُمْ}$$

$$\text{يُخْسِرُونَ . أَلَا يَظُنُّ أُولَٰئِكَ أَنَّهُم مَّبْعُوثُونَ . لِيَوْمٍ عَظِيمٍ . يَوْمَ يَقُومُ النَّاسُ لِرَبِّ}$$

$$\text{الْعَالَمِينَ}$$

20

"Woe to those who give less in measuring. Those who when they
have to receive by measure from men, demand full measures.
And when they have to give by measure or weight to (other)
men, they give less than due. Do they not think that they will be
resurrected (for reckoning) on a Great Day? The Day when all
mankind shall stand before the Lord of mankind." (83:1-6)

The command of maintaining justice in measurement has been
mentioned in many places of the Holy Qur'ān such as in Sūrah Al-
An'ām,

$$وَأَوْفُوا الْكَيْلَ وَالْمِيزَانَ بِالْقِسْطِ$$

"And give full measure and weight with justice." (6:152)

Also in Sūrah Banee Isrā'eel,

$$وَأَوْفُوا الْكَيْلَ إِذَا كِلْتُمْ وَزِنُوا بِالْقِسْطَاسِ الْمُسْتَقِيمِ ذَٰلِكَ خَيْرٌ وَأَحْسَنُ تَأْوِيلًا$$

"Measure in full when you measure and weigh with the proper
scale. This is best and better in the final outcome" (17:35)

Verses 10, 11, 12 and 13

$$وَالْأَرْضَ وَضَعَهَا لِلْأَنَامِ$$

"Allāh has placed the earth for people."

$$فِيهَا فَاكِهَةٌ وَالنَّخْلُ ذَاتُ الْأَكْمَامِ$$

"On it are fruit and palms with sheathed stalks."

21

وَالْحَبُّ ذُو الْعَصْفِ وَالرَّيْحَانُ

"Seeds as chaff and sustenance as well."

فَبِأَيِّ آلَاءِ رَبِّكُمَا تُكَذِّبَانِ

"So which favours of your Lord will the two of you
(man and Jinn) deny?"

Earth and its Fruits

The word انام (Anām) with a Fatha on the first letter, refers to all the creatures that are on the surface of the earth. Imām Baidāwi 🌸 translates the word as everything having a soul. The word Anām in this particular verse refers to mankind and Jinn because it is on-ly these two creations of Allāh 🌸 who are obliged to follow the laws of Shariah. The verse, **"So which favours of your Lord will the two of you (man and Jinn) deny?"** is repeated throughout the Sūrah constantly addressing mankind and Jinn with the pronouns and the dual forms of the verbs of His favours.

Allāh 🌸 has created the earth such that it is not too hard or too soft so we can tread upon it. It is not too hard so that mankind can dig the earth to construct dams, wells and graves and lay the founda-tions of buildings etc. At the same time, the earth can support con-structions, railways and motorways and enables man to utilize the resources of the earth. Allāh 🌸 makes a reference of this in Sūrah Al-Mulk,

22

هُوَ الَّذِي جَعَلَ لَكُمُ الْأَرْضَ ذَلُوْلًا فَامْشُوْا فِي مَنَاكِبِهَا وَكُلُوْا مِنْ رِزْقِهِ وَإِلَيْهِ النُّشُوْرُ

"It is He Who has made the earth submissive to you (i.e. easy to tread upon) so walk in its path and eat from its provision, and to Him will be the resurrection." (67:15)

In verse 11, Allāh ﷻ makes a reference to fruits, palms and sheathed stalks. The Arabic term used for fruits is 'Fākihah' which we eat normally for pleasure when dining. Allāh ﷻ has covered the stalks of such plants so that the fruits are protected and such coverings can be used for a variety of purposes. In addition to this, Allāh ﷻ has mentioned in verse twelve that He has created seeds as chaffs. This verse refers to cereals like wheat, barley, etc, which are like small seeds providing ample nourishment for mankind. Such foods are also protected in coverings that are separated as chaffs to nourish animals. This is another great bounty of Allāh ﷻ because mankind is in need of the nourishment of pure animals and their milk. Moreover, animals are used as a means of transportation to transport human beings from one place to another as well as carrying loads and luggage.

The word 'Ar-Rayhān' refers to fragrant flowers meaning that Allāh ﷻ has provided a variety of fragrances and sweet-smelling flowers. Sayyidunā Abdullāh Ibn Abbās ؓ translates it as sustenance and states that the word Rayhān implies to sustenance wherever it is mentioned in the Holy Qur'ān. This is because sustenance is something from which mankind derives satisfaction.

Allāh's ﷻ Countless Favours

After mentioning some of the blessings, Allāh ﷻ thereafter addresses mankind in a form of a question, **"So which favours of your Lord will the two of you (man and Jinn) deny?"** Mujāhid ﵀ and other scholars of the Holy Qur'ān have mentioned in regards to this verse that the bounties and favours (of Allāh ﷻ) are apparent to us whilst we are surrounded by them which we cannot deny. Therefore, we must say as the believers amongst the Jinns said, "O' Allāh ﷻ! None of Your favours do we deny and all praises are unto You." Sayyidunā Abdullāh Ibn Abbās ﵁ used to say, "Nay, our Lord!" meaning, "None of Your favours do we deny."

Verses 14, 15, 16

خَلَقَ الْإِنْسَانَ مِنْ صَلْصَالٍ كَالْفَخَّارِ

"Allāh created man from a melodious sounding sand that resembles potters clay."

وَخَلَقَ الْجَانَّ مِنْ مَّارِجٍ مِّنْ نَّارٍ

"And created Jinn from pure leaping fire."

فَبِأَيِّ آلَاءِ رَبِّكُمَا تُكَذِّبَانِ

"So which favours of your Lord will the two of you (man and Jinn) deny?"

Allāh ﷻ has created man from a melodious sounding sand that resembles potters clay. The word 'Insān' in this context refers

24

unanimously to Sayyidunā Ādam ﷺ. It is derived from the root word 'Uns' (affection). Thus, he has been termed 'Insān' because no man can live in isolation and man requires to co-exist with other people, sharing their affection. Another Arabic term used for man is 'Bashar'. The word literally means skin. It is used for man because unlike other animals, his skin is not completely covered in hair. Excluding his head, most of his skin on his body is visible.

The word 'Salsāl' (clay) refers to the wet soil when it becomes dry and heavy. The word 'Fakkhār' refers to the wet soil when it is baked.

Just as Sayyidunā Ādam ﷺ was the father of mankind, many scholars assert that Iblees was the father of Jinn. Therefore, it is often said that man in general is created from earth and that the Jinn are created from fire because their fathers were created from these substances.

In Sūrah Mu'min, it mentions that man was created from soil, while Sūrah Sād and Sūrah Al-Hijr mention that it was clay. In this Sūrah, Sūrah Ar-Rahmān, Allāh ﷻ says that He created man from a melodious sounding sand.

In actual fact, initially water was mixed with soil, turning it into clay. Then, this clay was left until it began to decompose and become dark in colour. Thereafter, the mould of Sayyidunā Ādam ﷺ was cast with this. When the mould set and dried, it became like potted clay that has a melodious sound when struck. The various verses of the Holy Qur'ān individually refer to these various stages in man's creation.

The blessing of being created and granted life is an extremely great bounty without which many other bounties cannot be enjoyed. Because Allāh ﷻ has granted these many favours to mankind and to Jinn, it is incumbent on them to be grateful to Him. Allāh ﷻ reminds them of this when He states, **"So which favours of your Lord do you two (man and Jinn) deny?"**

Mankind, having all these blessings still persists on disbelief. Allāh ﷻ astonishingly says,

$$\text{كَيْفَ تَكْفُرُونَ بِاللهِ وَكُنْتُمْ أَمْوَاتًا فَأَحْيَاكُمْ ثُمَّ يُمِيتُكُمْ ثُمَّ يُحْيِيكُمْ ثُمَّ إِلَيْهِ تُرْجَعُونَ}$$

"How can you disbelieve in Allāh when you were once lifeless and it was He Who granted you life? Thereafter, He will cause you to die and give you life and then, you will return to Him." (2:28)

In Sūrah Ibrāheem, Allāh ﷻ again reminds us of His blessings.

$$\text{اللهُ الَّذِي خَلَقَ السَّمَاوَاتِ وَالْأَرْضَ وَأَنْزَلَ مِنَ السَّمَاءِ مَاءً فَأَخْرَجَ بِهِ مِنَ الثَّمَرَاتِ رِزْقًا لَكُمْ وَسَخَّرَ لَكُمُ الْفُلْكَ لِتَجْرِيَ فِي الْبَحْرِ بِأَمْرِهِ وَسَخَّرَ لَكُمُ الْأَنْهَارَ. وَسَخَّرَ لَكُمُ الشَّمْسَ وَالْقَمَرَ دَائِبَيْنِ وَسَخَّرَ لَكُمُ اللَّيْلَ وَالنَّهَارَ. وَآتَاكُمْ مِنْ كُلِّ مَا سَأَلْتُمُوهُ}$$

وَإِن تَعُدُّواْ نِعْمَتَ اللَّهِ لَا تُحْصُوهَا إِنَّ الْإِنسَانَ لَظَلُومٌ كَفَّارٌ .

"Allāh ﷻ is He Who created the heavens and the earth and sends rain from the sky, thereby extracting fruits as sustenance for you. He placed the ships at your service so that they may travel over the oceans by His command and He subjugated the rivers for you. He also placed the sun and the moon at your service, the two being constantly in motion. He also placed the day and the night at your service. And (in addition to all this) He grants you whatever you ask of Him. If you try (repeatedly) to count Allāh's bounties, you will never be able to do so. Indeed, man is extremely unjust and very ungrateful." (14:32-34)

How beautifully and compassionately Allāh ﷻ proclaims in the Holy Qur'ān,

مَّا يَفْعَلُ اللَّهُ بِعَذَابِكُمْ إِن شَكَرْتُمْ وَآمَنتُمْ وَكَانَ اللَّهُ شَاكِرًا عَلِيمًا

"Why must Allāh punish you if you are grateful (for His favours to you) and have Imān. Allāh is Most Appreciative (of every good act and will reward you tremendously for it), All Knowing (all good is known to Him)." (4:147)

Verses 17 to 25

رَبُّ الْمَشْرِقَيْنِ وَرَبُّ الْمَغْرِبَيْنِ

"(Allāh) the Lord of the two easts and the two wests."

فَبِأَيِّ آلَاءِ رَبِّكُمَا تُكَذِّبَانِ

"So which of the favours of your Lord do the two of you deny?"

مَرَجَ الْبَحْرَيْنِ يَلْتَقِيَانِ

"He has released the two waters so that they meet."

بَيْنَهُمَا بَرْزَخٌ لَّا يَبْغِيَانِ

"Between the two waters is a barrier so that the two do not transgress."

فَبِأَيِّ آلَاءِ رَبِّكُمَا تُكَذِّبَانِ

"So which of the favours of your Lord do the two of you deny?"

يَخْرُجُ مِنْهُمَا اللُّؤْلُؤُ وَالْمَرْجَانُ

"Pearls and corals emerge from both of them."

فَبِأَيِّ آلَاءِ رَبِّكُمَا تُكَذِّبَانِ

"So which of the favours of your Lord do the two of you deny?"

وَلَهُ الْجَوَارِ الْمُنْشَآتُ فِي الْبَحْرِ كَالْأَعْلَامِ

"His are the raised ships on the oceans like mountains."

فَبِأَيِّ آلَاءِ رَبِّكُمَا تُكَذِّبَانِ

"So which of the favours of your Lord do the two of you deny?"

Great Oceans and Seas

Allāh ﷻ is the Lord of the two easts and the two wests. The easts refer to the rising points of the sun while the wests refer to the setting points of the sun. The rising and setting of the sun determines the day and the night, both of which are beneficial to man and Jinn.

Sayyidunā Abdullāh Ibn Abbās ﷺ narrates that the two easts refer to the point where the sun rises during Summer and the point where it rises during Winter. Similarly, the two wests refer to the point where the sun sets during Summer and the point where it sets during the Winter.

Allāh ﷻ further says, **"He has released the two waters so that they meet."** Literally, the verb 'Maraja' means to let loose. The word 'Bahrain' (two seas or two types of water) refers to sweet and salty waters. Allāh ﷻ has created two types of water. In some places the two seas meet together, the samples of which are available in every region of the world. However, where the sweet and salty water meet, there is a distinct barrier between the sweet and salty waters. In some cases, the two types of water are seen distinctly in higher or lower positions. If the salty water overrides the sweet water, the characteristics of the sweet water will not be spoiled, nor will the characteristics of the salty water be affected in any way if the sweet water overrides it.

Thus, the Holy Qur'ān amazingly says,

29

بَيْنَهُمَا بَرْزَخٌ لَّا يَبْغِيَانِ

"He has set forth the two seas that meet together, while between
them there is a barrier which they do not transgress." (55:20)

Man and Jinn derive various benefits from the two types of water
and therefore are obliged to express gratitude to Allāh ﷻ. Allāh ﷻ
reminds them of this when He says, **"So which of the favours of
your Lord do the two of you deny?"**
"Pearls and corals emerge from both of them." The various jew-
els that emerge from the sea are also a great favour from Allāh ﷻ
and man and Jinn are required to be grateful to Allāh ﷻ for these.
Allāh ﷻ reiterates, **"So which of the favours of your Lord do the
two of you deny?"**

Sayyidunā Abdullāh Ibn Abbās ؓ states that the Arabic word
'Lu'lu,' translated above as pearls refers to smaller pearls and the
word 'Marjān,' translated above as coral refers to larger pearls.

Allāh ﷻ explains the two types of water in more detail in Sūrah Al-
Furqān where He states,

وَهُوَ الَّذِي مَرَجَ الْبَحْرَيْنِ هَذَا عَذْبٌ فُرَاتٌ وَهَذَا مِلْحٌ أُجَاجٌ وَجَعَلَ بَيْنَهُمَا بَرْزَخًا
وَحِجْرًا مَحْجُورًا

"It is He Who has merged two seas, the one being sweet and
quenching, while the other is salty and bitter. He has created between them a barrier that acts as a veil." (25:53)

Allāh 🕌 goes on to say, **"His are the raised ships on the oceans like mountains."** These huge ships remain afloat only by Allāh's 🕌 will. When water gets rough and strong winds blow, it is only Allāh 🕌 that protects the ship and those in the ship. Allāh 🕌 allows the large ships laden with hundreds of tons of cargo to traverse through the seas and oceans so that men may transport goods from one continent to another.

In Sūrah Al-Baqarah, He also mentions about this blessing of the huge ships which traverse the oceans carrying goods of benefit to men.

The word 'Jawāriy' is the plural of 'Jāriyah.' One of its meanings is ship and that is the sense in which it is used in the current verse.

Allāh's 🕌 Countenance

Verses 26, 27and 28

كُلُّ مَنْ عَلَيْهَا فَانٍ

"Everything on earth shall perish."

وَيَبْقَى وَجْهُ رَبِّكَ ذُو الْجَلَالِ وَالْإِكْرَامِ

"Only the Countenance of your Lord, the Possessor of majesty
and benevolence shall remain."

31

فَبِأَيِّ آلَاءِ رَبِّكُمَا تُكَذِّبَانِ

"So which favours of your Lord do the two of you deny?"

"Everything on earth shall perish." Everyone who lives on it has to perish and your Lord's Countenance will remain, full of majesty, full of honour.

As Muslims, we believe that Allāh 🕮 is Eternal. Allāh 🕮 says,

هُوَ الْأَوَّلُ وَالْآخِرُ وَالظَّاهِرُ وَالْبَاطِنُ وَهُوَ بِكُلِّ شَيْءٍ عَلِيمٌ

"He is the First (nothing is before Him) and the Last (nothing is after Him), the Most High (nothing is above Him) and the Most Near (nothing is nearer than Him) and He is the All-Knower of everything." (57:3)

The Holy Qur'ān emphasises this point and to be the First is absolute, in that it has no limit beyond it in the beginning. Therefore, there is no beginning for Allāh 🕮. To be the Last is specific, in that it is something which has no limit in ending, it is something which is Everlasting. This demonstrates the continuity of His existence. In another verse, Allāh 🕮 says,

كُلُّ شَيْءٍ هَالِكٌ إِلَّا وَجْهَهُ

"Everything shall perish but His Countenance." (28:88)

Indeed, existence and Allāh's 🕮 Being are necessary corollaries. It is not possible that the quality of existence be separated from Him and that non-existence is associated with Him. His existence is always necessary and His eradication is impossible.

In the verse, the word 'Jalāl' (translated as Majesty) refers to Allāh's ﷻ grandeur and greatness and 'Al-Ikrām' (translated as Benevolence) means that Allāh ﷻ should be revered and honoured to the extent that no degree of Shirk (polytheism) is perpetrated. Viewing the word 'Al-Ikrām' from a different perspective, other commentators have mentioned that it means that Allāh ﷻ is the only One Who can truly bestow favours and mercy on the creation.

Allāh ﷻ states in Sūrah Al-Fajr,

$$فَأَمَّا الْإِنْسَانُ إِذَا مَا ابْتَلَاهُ رَبُّهُ فَأَكْرَمَهُ وَنَعَّمَهُ فَيَقُولُ رَبِّي أَكْرَمَنِ$$

"As for man, when his Lord tries him by granting honour and favours, he says, 'My Lord has honoured me.'" (89:15)

Allāh ﷻ says in Sūrah Banee Isrāeel, **"When We bestow favours upon men, he turns away and changing direction, goes far."** (17:83)

It is stated in 'Faydhul Qadeer': The special honour denoted by the word Ikram is not granted to sinners. However, general favours are granted to the disbelievers as well, as it is mentioned in one particular verse, **"Say (O Muhammad), 'Who has forbidden the adornment with clothes given by Allāh which He has produced for His servants and all kind of lawful things of food?' Say, They are in the life of this world for those who believe, (and)** exclusively for them (believers) on the Day of Resurrection (the disbelievers will not share them).'" (7:32)

Therefore, we deduce from this verse that the disbelievers are benefiting from the bounties of Allāh ﷻ due to the believers even in this world, but in the Hereafter the disbelievers will be deprived of all favours.

Allāh ﷻ created us as Ashraful-Makhlooqāt (the best of creation), hence, every human being is blessed with a degree of honour and respect by simply being human. This is categorically mentioned in verse 70 of Sūrah Banee Isrā'eel where Allāh ﷻ says,

وَلَقَدْ كَرَّمْنَا بَنِي آدَمَ وَحَمَلْنَاهُمْ فِي الْبَرِّ وَالْبَحْرِ وَرَزَقْنَاهُم مِّنَ الطَّيِّبَاتِ وَفَضَّلْنَاهُمْ
عَلَى كَثِيرٍ مِّمَّنْ خَلَقْنَا تَفْضِيلًا

"We have granted honour to the children of Ādam and We have carried them on land and sea, and have provided them with lawful good things and have preferred them above many of those whom We have created with a marked preference." (17:70)

However, for the disbelievers, this honour is restricted to this world. As soon as they die, they will be made to suffer disgrace that will continue throughout eternity.

In the Hereafter, the disbelievers will have neither honour nor favours, whereas the believers shall enjoy an abundance of both. In the verse, **"Only the Countenance of your Lord." (55:27)** The word

Wajh (face) according to the majority of the commentators, stands for the Being of Allāh ﷾. The attached second person pronoun in Rabbi-ka (your Lord) refers to the Messenger of Allāh ﷺ. It is a great honour for him that he should be remembered by Allāh ﷾ in special ways when praising him, as for instance, Abduhū (His servant). Here Allāh ﷾, the Lord of the lords, declares His direct special relationship with the Holy Prophet ﷺ and addresses him with Rabbi-ka (your Lord).

Allāh ﷾ mentions two of His special attributes in this verse, i.e. Dhul-Jalāli wal-Ikrām. Imām Tirmizi ﵀ and Imām Nasai ﵀, as well as Imām Ahmad Ibn Hanbal ﵀, relate that Sayyidunā Ibn Āmir ﵁ has narrated that the Holy Prophet ﷺ said, "Persist in invoking Allāh ﷾ with يَا ذَالْجَلَالِ وَالْإِكْرَامِ (O' Lōrd of Majesty and Honour)."

Allāh's ﷾ Majesty

Verses 29 and 30

يَسْأَلُهُ مَنْ فِي السَّمَاوَاتِ وَالْأَرْضِ كُلَّ يَوْمٍ هُوَ فِي شَأْنٍ

"All in the heavens and the earth ask from Him and He is engaged in some matter every day."

فَبِأَيِّ آلَاءِ رَبِّكُمَا تُكَذِّبَانِ

"So which favours of your Lord do the two of you deny?"

n this verse, Allāh ﷾ affirms that He is Independent, free of all needs from anyone else and that all creatures stand in need of Him in all conditions and situations. They all seek His help willingly or unwillingly. The worldly creatures ask for their specific needs. In this world, they need sustenance, health, wealth and comfort whilst in the Hereafter, they need forgiveness, mercy and Paradise.

The celestial creations (angels) do not eat and drink. They do however need Allāh's ﷻ mercy and grace. His mercy, grace and forgiveness surrounds them all the time. In the phrase 'every day', the word day is not used in its popular sense, but in the sense of 'time' in general. All His creation in different parts of the world, in different languages, supplicate for their needs all the time. Obviously, each individual and every creation has countless needs. So, who else besides Allāh ﷻ is able to respond to their needs every moment of the time?

Therefore, 'every day' is preceded by the sentence, He is engaged in some matter, that is, His attributes know no limit or count and keep finding their manifestations in diverse ways all the time. He gives life to some and causes others to die. He elevates some and others He degrades. He alleviates the adversity of some, He causes the aggrieved ones to smile, He grants the requests of supplicants, He forgives the sins of the sinners and makes them deserving of Paradise. He gives power to some and He snatches it away from others. In short, every attribute of Allāh ﷻ keeps finding its manifestation in diverse ways all the time.

Man and Jinn

Verses 31 and 32

سَنَفْرُغُ لَكُمْ أَيُّهَ الثَّقَلَانِ

"We shall soon free Ourselves for you, O' the two of you groups."

فَبِأَيِّ آلَاءِ رَبِّكُمَا تُكَذِّبَانِ

"So which favours of your Lord do the two of you deny?"

Verse 31 is symbolic and does not mean that Allāh ﷻ is too preoccupied with other duties to take reckoning. Allāh ﷻ is capable of doing everything perfectly at once and no act will hinder Him from accomplishing another. The symbolic reference is to emphasise the fact that reckoning will be meticulous.

This type of speech pattern is common in the Arabic language. For example one would say, "I shall attend to you", even when one is not busy with anything.

Allāh ﷻ says, **"O' the two of you groups."** Referring to the human beings and the Jinns, as in the Hadeeth, "Everyone will be able to hear it except the Thaqalain (human and Jinns)."

In another narration, it explains the word Thaqalain. The Holy Prophet ﷺ said, "Except mankind and Jinn." Allāh ﷻ says, **"Then which of the blessings of your Lord will you both deny?"**

37

<u>Verses 33 and 34</u>

يَا مَعْشَرَ الْجِنِّ وَالْإِنسِ إِنِ اسْتَطَعْتُمْ أَن تَنفُذُوا مِنْ أَقْطَارِ السَّمَاوَاتِ وَالْأَرْضِ فَانفُذُوا ۚ لَا تَنفُذُونَ إِلَّا بِسُلْطَانٍ

"O assembly of Jinn and man. If you are able to transcend the limits of the heavens and the earth, then do so. You will be unable to transcend without the power."

فَبِأَيِّ آلَاءِ رَبِّكُمَا تُكَذِّبَانِ

"So which favours of your Lord do the two of you deny?"

Verse 33 addresses mankind and Jinns clearly informing us that we will never be able to escape Allāh's ﷻ orders and decrees because they encompass us.

We will never be able to avoid or avert His rule and judgement over us. We are surrounded by it wherever we may be. This is also about the gathering when the angels, comprising seven lines in every direction will surround the creation. None of the creation will be able to escape on that Day.

Allāh ﷻ paints the picture of the Day of Judgement in many places of the Holy Qur'ān. In Sūrah Al-Fajr, Allāh ﷻ says,

وَجَاءَ رَبُّكَ وَالْمَلَكُ صَفًّا صَفًّا ۚ وَجِيءَ يَوْمَئِذٍ بِجَهَنَّمَ ۚ يَوْمَئِذٍ يَتَذَكَّرُ الْإِنسَانُ وَأَنَّىٰ لَهُ الذِّكْرَىٰ.

"And your Lord will come with angels in rows. And Hell will be brought near that Day. On that Day will men remember, but how will that remembrance (then) avail him? He will say: Alas! Would that I had sent forth (good deeds) for my life." (89:22-23)

In Sūrah Al-Qiyāmah Allāh ﷻ says,

$$
\text{يَقُولُ الْإِنْسَانُ يَوْمَئِذٍ أَيْنَ الْمَفَرُّ . كَلَّا لَا وَزَرَ .}
$$

$$
\text{إِلَى رَبِّكَ يَوْمَئِذٍ الْمُسْتَقَرُّ .}
$$

"On that Day men will say: 'Where (is the refuge) to flee?' No! There is no refuge! Onto your Lord will be the place of rest that Day." (75:10-12)

In Sūrah An-Naba, Allāh ﷻ says,

$$
\text{يَوْمَ يَقُومُ الرُّوحُ وَالْمَلَائِكَةُ صَفًّا لَّا يَتَكَلَّمُونَ إِلَّا مَنْ أَذِنَ لَهُ الرَّحْمَنُ وَقَالَ صَوَابًا .}
$$

$$
\text{ذَلِكَ الْيَوْمُ الْحَقُّ فَمَن شَاءَ اتَّخَذَ إِلَى رَبِّهِ مَآبًا . إِنَّا أَنذَرْنَاكُمْ عَذَابًا قَرِيبًا يَوْمَ}
$$

$$
\text{يَنظُرُ الْمَرْءُ مَا قَدَّمَتْ يَدَاهُ وَيَقُولُ الْكَافِرُ يَا لَيْتَنِي كُنتُ تُرَابًا .}
$$

"The Day Ar-Rooh (Jibreel) and the angels will stand forth in rows, they will not speak except him whom the Most Gracious (Allāh) allows and he will speak what is right. That is (without doubt) the True Day, so whosoever wills, let him seek a place with (or a way to) his Lord (by obeying) Him in this worldly life. Verily, We have warned you of a near torment the Day when man will see that (the deeds) which his hands have sent forth and the disbeliever will say: Woe to me! Would that I were dust!" (78:38-40)

39

This verse shows that even the combined forces of men and Jinn cannot control or transcend the limits of the heavens and the earth. Since men and Jinn are helpless in this very world, they will surely be powerless in the Hereafter as well. It is therefore useless thinking that one will be able to escape Allāh's ﷻ punishment as there is nowhere to hide. When the Day of Judgement arrives, every person will realise the error of his ways. However, it will then be too late. It is a great favour from Allāh ﷻ that He has forewarned men and Jinn about this inevitable Day.

"So which favours of your Lord do the two of you deny?"

Horrors of Judgement Day

In Tafseer Rūhul-Ma'āni, it states: If the purpose of penetrating through the heavens and the earth mentioned in the verse is to escape death, then it refers to this world and means, It is not within the power of any man or Jinn to cross the bounds of the heavens and earth to escape death. This is stated according to human thinking. In reality no one is outside the power and the authority of Allāh ﷻ, even if he crosses the bounds of the heavens and the earth. If the escape intended by penetrating through the heavens and the earth stands for escaping accountability on the Day of Judgement, the purpose of the verse is to demonstrate its absolute impossibility.

According to other Qur'anic verses and Ahādeeth, the heaven will crack open on the Day of Judgement, and all the angels will border on the sides of the earth and the people will be besieged from all sides. The Jinns and human beings will experience the horrors of the Day of Judgement and run in different directions. In whichever direction they run, the angels will lay siege to those areas that Allāh ﷻ has fortified for the purpose of recapturing the escapees.

Verses 35 and 36

يُرْسَلُ عَلَيْكُمَا شُوَاظٌ مِّن نَّارٍ وَّنُحَاسٌ فَلَا تَنتَصِرَانِ

"A flame and smoke shall be unleashed on the two of you (man and Jinn) and you will be helpless to ward it off."

فَبِأَيِّ آلَاءِ رَبِّكُمَا تُكَذِّبَانِ

"So which of the favours of your Lord do the two of you deny?"

In the above verse, Allāh ﷻ describes the horrors of Qiyāmah so that people may refrain from Kufr (disbelief) and become sincere Muslims.

Allāh ﷻ says in Sūrah Al-Mursalāt that the people of Jahannam will be told,

اِنطَلِقُوٓا إِلَىٰ ظِلٍّ ذِي ثَلَاثِ شُعَبٍ
لَّا ظَلِيلٍ وَّلَا يُغْنِي مِنَ اللَّهَبِ ۚ إِنَّهَا تَرْمِي بِشَرَرٍ كَالْقَصْرِ ۚ كَأَنَّهُ جِمَالَتٌ صُفْرٌ ۚ وَيْلٌ
يَوْمَئِذٍ لِّلْمُكَذِّبِينَ

"Proceed towards the canopy of these parts which will neither provide shade nor offer shelter against the heat. Indeed, Jahannam throws sparks like huge palaces resembling pitch black

41

**camels. May destruction be the end for the deniers on that day."
(77:30-34)**

These verses of Sūrah Al-Mursalāt state that the smoke of Jahan-nam shall assume the appearance of a canopy. Whereas the cano-pies of this world offer protection from heat, the smoke canopy of Jahannam will offer no such protection, even though it will be ex-tremely dark. None shall be able to assist another.

Sayyidunā Abdullāh Ibn Abbās ﷺ and other commentators have said that the word 'Shuwāz' refers to the flame of the fire without smoke and the word 'Nuhās' refers to smoke in which there is no flame.

This verse also addresses the two species of creation, the Jinns and mankind. It addresses them and describes how fire and smoke will be unleashed against them. The verse could mean that after the reckoning is over and the disbelievers are sent to Hell, they will experience two different types of punishment. On some places there will be just fire and flame with no smoke at all. In other plac-es there will be smoke and no fire or flame.

Other commentators regard this verse as a supplement to the pro-ceeding one, and assign the following meaning to it: O' Jinn and mankind, it is not within your power to cross the bounds of the heavens. If you do attempt to escape on the Day of Resurrection, the angels (including those guarding the Hell-Fire) will bring you back by directing the flames of fire and smoke.

The verb 'Falā Tantasirān' is derived from 'Intisār' which means to help someone or to defend him against a calamity and thus the words 'Falā Tantasirān' signify that the Jinns and mankind will not be able to help each other against Divine punishment, try as they might.

Verses 37 and 38

فَإِذَا انْشَقَّتِ السَّمَاءُ فَكَانَتْ وَرْدَةً كَالدِّهَانِ

"The time shall certainly come when the sky shall cleave asunder and become red like hide."

فَبِأَيِّ آلَاءِ رَبِّكُمَا تُكَذِّبَانِ

"So which of the favours of your Lord do the two of you deny?"

This verse is referring to the horrors of the Day of Resurrection. Allāh ﷻ has mentioned in numerous verses the catastrophic scenes of Judgement Day. In a particular verse, Allāh ﷻ says,

وَانْشَقَّتِ السَّمَاءُ فَهِيَ يَوْمَئِذٍ وَاهِيَةٌ

"And the sky will split and become weak that day." (69:16)

In another place, Allāh ﷻ says,

وَيَوْمَ تَشَقَّقُ السَّمَاءُ بِالْغَمَامِ وَنُزِّلَ الْمَلَائِكَةُ تَنْزِيلًا

"And (remember) the Day when the heaven shall be render asunder with clouds and the angels will be sent down with a grand descending." (25:25)

43

In Sūrah Al-Inshiqāq, Allāh ﷻ says,

إِذَا السَّمَاءُ انْشَقَّتْ . وَأَذِنَتْ لِرَبِّهَا وَحُقَّتْ

"When the heaven is split asunder and listens to and obeys its
Lord; and it must do so." (84:1-2)

"It becomes red like hide," means they will melt just as sediment
and silver are melted when heated and they will be coloured just
as dyes stain something; sometimes red, sometimes yellow, blue or
green. This demonstrates the extent of the horrors of the mighty
Day of Resurrection.

The famous commentator, As-Suddi ﷺ said, "It will be like a rosy
colour and like stained oil." Imām Mujāhid ﷺ says, "Like the colours of dyes."

Man's Desperation
Verses 39 to 45

فَيَوْمَئِذٍ لَا يُسْأَلُ عَن ذَنبِهِ إِنسٌ وَلَا جَانٌّ

"On that day, no man and no Jinn shall be asked about his sins."

فَبِأَيِّ آلَاءِ رَبِّكُمَا تُكَذِّبَانِ

"So which favours of your Lord do the two of you deny?"

يُعْرَفُ الْمُجْرِمُونَ بِسِيمَاهُمْ فَيُؤْخَذُ بِالنَّوَاصِي وَالْأَقْدَامِ

"The criminals will be recognised by their traits and will be
seized by their foreheads and feet."

فَبِأَيِّ آلَاءِ رَبِّكُمَا تُكَذِّبَانِ

"So which of the favours of your Lord do the two of you deny?"

هٰذِهِ جَهَنَّمُ الَّتِي يُكَذِّبُ بِهَا الْمُجْرِمُونَ

"This is Jahannam which the criminals used to deny."

يَطُوفُونَ بَيْنَهَا وَبَيْنَ حَمِيمٍ آنٍ

"They shall pass between it and the boiling water."

فَبِأَيِّ آلَاءِ رَبِّكُمَا تُكَذِّبَانِ

"So which of the favours of your Lord do the two of you deny?"

On that Day no man and no Jinn shall be asked about his sins. A person is questioned to ascertain facts because the questioner is unaware regarding the truth of a matter.

However, questions are sometimes posed merely to remind the person being asked about some certain acts. Allāh ﷻ is aware of every person's acts and has no need to ask them what they did in the world. Their questioning will therefore, not be to establish whether they did something or not, but it will be to remind them of their misdeeds.

Allāh ﷻ says in Sūrah Al-Qasas,

وَلَا يُسْأَلُ عَنْ ذُنُوبِهِمُ الْمُجْرِمُونَ

"The criminals will not be questioned about their sins." (28:78)

The guilty ones shall be forced to admit their misdeeds on the Day of Judgement and they will be unable to deny anything.
Allāh ﷻ says in Sūrah Al-A'rāf,

فَلَنَسْأَلَنَّ الَّذِينَ أُرْسِلَ إِلَيْهِمْ وَلَنَسْأَلَنَّ الْمُرْسَلِينَ . فَلَنَقُصَّنَّ عَلَيْهِمْ بِعِلْمٍ وَمَا كُنَّا غَائِبِينَ

"We shall definitely question those to whom Messengers were sent and We will surely question the Messengers. We will certainly narrate to them with knowledge and We were not absent." (7:6-7)

This event will take place when people will have given account of their deeds, and judgement will have been passed against the criminals to go to Hell on the Day of Reckoning. They will not be questioned nor will any negotiation be held about their sins at that stage.

Testimonies of the Organs

The criminals' characteristic signs will be seen on their faces and they will be thrown into Hell accordingly. According to the great commentator Qatādah ﷺ, this refers to a stage after they will have refused under oath. Then their mouths and tongues will be sealed and their hands and feet will be asked to bear witness. At that stage, no more questions will be asked from them.

In Sūrah Yāseen, Allāh ﷻ mentions this very clearly,

اَلْيَوْمَ نَخْتِمُ عَلَى أَفْوَاهِهِمْ وَتُكَلِّمُنَا أَيْدِيهِمْ وَتَشْهَدُ أَرْجُلُهُمْ بِمَا كَانُوا يَكْسِبُونَ

"On this Day, We shall seal their mouths. Their hands shall
speak to Us and their legs will testify to what they earned (the
sins they committed)." (36:65)

In Sūrah Hā Meem Sajdah, Allāh ﷻ describes the agony of the disbelievers:

"(Do not forget) The Day when Allāh's enemies will be gathered
(and driven) towards the fire and (because of their large numbers, they will have to be) restrained (so that order is maintained). (This will continue) until when they arrive there
(Jahannam), their ears, eyes and skins will testify (against them)
about what (actions) they did (in the world). (When their skins
begin to testify to the evil acts that they have witnessed them doing), they will say to their skins (and to the other limbs that will
testify against them), 'Why do you testify (bear witness) against
us (when we did these acts for your pleasure as well)?' They
(their skins and other limbs) will reply, 'Allāh Who gives speech
to everything has enabled us to speak. It was He Who created
you the first time and to Him is your return.'" (41:19-21)
Addressing these people on the Day of Judgement, Allāh ﷻ will
say,

"You did not hide (your actions, little imagining) that your ears,
eyes and skin will testify against you (as you now see them doing), but (even worse than this) you (foolishly) thought that
Allāh is unaware of most of the things you do. That was the per-

ception that you held about your Lord which has destroyed you and made you among the losers (the disbelievers). (41:22-23)

"The criminals will be recognised by their traits." The traits that they will be recognised by are mentioned in Sūrah Banū Isrāeel in the following words,

$$وَنَحْشُرُهُمْ يَوْمَ الْقِيَامَةِ عَلَى وُجُوهِهِمْ عُمْيًا وَبُكْمًا وَصُمًّا$$

"We shall raise them on their faces on the Day of Judgement blind, dumb and deaf." (17:97)

Another trait is mentioned in Sūrah Tā Hā,

$$يَوْمَ يُنْفَخُ فِي الصُّورِ وَنَحْشُرُ الْمُجْرِمِينَ يَوْمَئِذٍ زُرْقًا . يَتَخَافَتُونَ بَيْنَهُمْ إِنْ لَبِثْتُمْ$$
$$إِلَّا عَشْرًا .$$

"The Day when the trumpet will be blown and the criminals shall be gathered with (frightened) blue eyes. They will whisper to each other saying, 'You have lived only for ten days'." (20:102-103)

Hell
Definition of Jahannam

The meaning of Jahannam is a deep place. Hell is also very deep and distant, hence, the Arabic name. It is also one of the names of the fire in which Allāh ﷻ will punish the disobedient, the disbelievers and the polytheists.

Hell is the worst possible place for the disbelievers. Numerous types of punishments will be given to the disobedient. The details of the horrific punishments are mentioned in the different verses of the Holy Qur'ān and Ahādeeth.

Depth of Hell

Sayyidunā Abū Mūsā Al-Ash'ari ؓ narrates that the Holy Prophet ﷺ said (whilst describing the depth of Hell), "If a stone is dropped into Hell, it will keep on falling for seventy years before reaching the bottom of Hell." (Ibn Hibbān)

Sayyidunā Abū Hurairah ؓ narrates, "Once we were sitting in the company of the Holy Prophet ﷺ, when we heard the sound of a falling object. Thereupon, the Holy Prophet ﷺ said, "Do you know what sound it is?"

"Allāh ﷻ and His Messenger ﷺ know best," we said. "This is a stone which was dropped by Allāh ﷻ from the mouth of Hell and it has now reached the bottom after continuous falling for seventy years; it was the sound of the falling of the same stone." (Muslim)

49

Walls of Hell

The Holy Prophet 🪷 is reported to have said, "Four walls are surrounding Hell. The width of every wall is a distance of 40 years of walking."

Gates of Hell

Allāh 🪷 describes the gates of Hell in these words,

وَإِنَّ جَهَنَّمَ لَمَوْعِدُهُمْ أَجْمَعِينَ . لَهَا سَبْعَةُ أَبْوَابٍ لِكُلِّ بَابٍ مِّنْهُمْ جُزْءٌ مَّقْسُومٌ .

"Verily Hell is the promised abode for them all! Belonging to it are seven gates; for each of these gates is a (special) class (of sinners) assigned." (15:43-44)

In a Hadeeth it is mentioned, "Hell has seven gates; one of them is for one who draws a sword against my Ummah." (Mishkāt)

Hāfiz Ibn Katheer 🪷, commenting on this verse said, "Each gate has been allotted its share of the followers of Iblees who will enter it and they will not be able to avoid it. May Allāh 🪷 protect us from it. Each will enter a gate according to his deeds and will be assigned a level of Hell according to his deeds."

When the disbelievers will be brought to Hell, its gates will be opened. And they will enter to remain there forever.

وَسِيقَ الَّذِينَ كَفَرُوا إِلَى جَهَنَّمَ زُمَرًا حَتَّى إِذَا جَاءُوهَا فُتِحَتْ أَبْوَابُهَا وَقَالَ لَهُمْ
خَزَنَتُهَا أَلَمْ يَأْتِكُمْ رُسُلٌ مِنْكُمْ يَتْلُونَ عَلَيْكُمْ آيَاتِ رَبِّكُمْ وَيُنْذِرُونَكُمْ لِقَاءَ
يَوْمِكُمْ هَذَا قَالُوا بَلَى وَلَكِنْ حَقَّتْ كَلِمَةُ الْعَذَابِ عَلَى الْكَافِرِينَ

"And those who disbelieved will be driven to Hell in groups,
until when they reach it, the gates thereof will be opened
(suddenly like a prison at the arrival of the prisoners), and its
keepers will say, 'Did not the Messengers come to you from
yourselves, reciting to you the verses of your Lord and warning
you of the meeting of this Day of yours?' They will say,
"Certainly! However (we failed to heed their advice because we
died as disbelievers so) the decision of punishment has passed
against the disbelievers.'" (39:71)

قِيلَ ادْخُلُوا أَبْوَابَ جَهَنَّمَ خَالِدِينَ فِيهَا فَبِئْسَ مَثْوَى الْمُتَكَبِّرِينَ

"It will be said (to them), 'Enter the gates of Jahannam where
you will live forever. Evil indeed is the abode of the arro-
gant.'" (39:72)

The Fire of Hell

The Holy Prophet ﷺ said, "Hell was inflamed for one thousand
years and its fire turned red. It was then inflamed for another one
thousand years and it became white. It was again inflamed for one
thousand years and it turned black. At present, Hell looks black
and dark." (Tirmizi)

Sayyidunā Abū Hurairah ﷺ narrates that the Holy Prophet ﷺ has said, "Your worldly fire is a seventieth part of the Fire of Hell." It was said to him, "O Messenger of Allāh ﷺ, this fire was sufficient (why is more needed?)" He replied, "The Fire of Hell is sixty-nine times sterner than this fire; each part is like the fire of this world." The scholars have said that the use of the number seventy in Arabic does not confine it to this number, but by saying seventy or a hundred the meaning is numerous and the expression is used to show excess in number. It is common sense that the Fire of Allāh ﷺ will be harsher and sharper than the fire of the world so that there may be a visible difference in the punishment meted out by Allāh ﷺ. Allāh ﷺ has made the fire of this world an example of this punishment.

Imām Ghazāli ﷺ has written that there is no comparison between the Fire of Hell and the fire of the world, but because the sternest punishment awarded in the world is through fire, it is mentioned as an example. If the fire of this world were presented before the inmates of Hell, they would jump into the worldly fire to protect themselves from the Fire of Hell. Allāh ﷺ describes the condition of the people of Hell,

$$\text{وَأَصْحَابُ الشِّمَالِ مَا أَصْحَابُ الشِّمَالِ . فِى سَمُوْمٍ وَّحَمِيْمٍ . وَّظِلٍّ مِّنْ يَّحْمُوْمٍ . لَا بَارِدٍ وَّلَا كَرِيْمٍ}$$

"And those on the left hand; who will be those on the left hand? In fierce hot wind and boiling water and a shadow of black smoke, (that shadow) neither cool, nor (even) pleasant."
(56:41-44)

The above verses include the things that people use in this world to comfort themselves when it is too hot. These three things are: water, air and shade. However, the verses state that these things will be of no help whatsoever to the people of Hell. The air of Hell is 'Samoom' which is an intensely hot wind, its water is 'Hameem', boiling water and its shade is 'Yahmoom', which is a part of the smoke of Hell.

Allāh ﷻ explains how strong this fire is, and how it affects the tormented,

$$\text{سَأُصْلِيهِ سَقَرَ . وَمَآ أَدْرَاكَ مَا سَقَرُ . لَا تُبْقِي وَلَا تَذَرُ .}$$
$$\text{لَوَّاحَةٌ لِّلْبَشَرِ}$$

"Soon I will cast him into the Hell-Fire. And what will explain to you exactly what Hell-Fire is? It spares not (any sinner) nor does it leave (anything unburnt). Burning and blackening the skins." (74:26-29)

The Fire will destroy everything and leave nothing untouched. It will burn skin, reaching to the bone, melt the contents of the stomach, mount to the heart and expose what is innermost.

The Fire of Hell never dies down, no matter how much time passes.

$$\text{فَذُوقُوا فَلَنْ نَّزِيدَكُمْ إِلَّا عَذَابًا}$$

"So taste (the results of your evil actions) no increase shall We give you, except torment." (78:30)

The Fire of Hell is rekindled every day, as it is stated in the Hadeeth reported by Muslim, "Pray Fajr Salāh, then stop praying when the sun is rising until it is fully up, for it rises between the horns of Shaytān and the disbelievers prostrate to the sun at that time. Then pray, for the prayer is witnessed (by the angels) until the shadow becomes the length of a lance. Then cease prayer, for at that time, Hell is heated up. Thereafter when the shadow moves forward, pray again."

Imām Bukhāri ☙ and Imām Muslim ☙ report from Sayyidunā Abū Hurairah ☙ that the Holy Prophet ☙ said, "When it becomes very hot, wait until it cools down to pray, because the intense heat is a breeze from Hell."

The Fire of Hell will be further refuelled on the Day of Resurrection when it receives its inhabitants.

$$\text{وَإِذَا الْجَحِيْمُ سُعِّرَتْ . وَإِذَا الْجَنَّةُ أُزْلِفَتْ}$$

"And when Hell-Fire shall be kindled to a fierce blaze and when Paradise shall be brought near." (81:12-13)

The People of Hell

The people of Hell, who will abide therein forever never leaving it and never dying, are the disbelievers and polytheists.

Allāh ﷻ mentions the disbelievers in numerous verses.

وَالَّذِينَ كَفَرُوا وَكَذَّبُوا بِآيَاتِنَا أُولَٰئِكَ أَصْحَابُ النَّارِ هُمْ فِيهَا خَالِدُونَ

"Those who reject faith and deny Our signs, they shall be the companions of the Fire; they shall abide therein." (2:39)

Regarding the polytheists, the Holy Qur'ān states,

مَا كَانَ لِلْمُشْرِكِينَ أَنْ يَعْمُرُوا مَسَاجِدَ اللهِ شَاهِدِينَ عَلَى أَنْفُسِهِمْ بِالْكُفْرِ أُولَٰئِكَ حَبِطَتْ أَعْمَالُهُمْ وَفِي النَّارِ هُمْ خَالِدُونَ

"It is not for the polytheists to attend the Houses of Allāh when they testify to disbelief against themselves. The works of such are in vain and in Fire shall they abide." (9:17)

Allāh ﷻ describes the plight of the disbelievers and polytheists,

يُرِيدُونَ أَنْ يَخْرُجُوا مِنَ النَّارِ وَمَا هُمْ بِخَارِجِينَ مِنْهَا وَلَهُمْ عَذَابٌ مُقِيمٌ

"They will try to get out of the fire but never will they get out from there. For them will be a permanent punishment ." (5:37)

Imām Bukhāri ﷺ narrates from Sayyidunā Umar ﷺ that the Holy

Prophet ﷺ said, "The people of Paradise will enter Paradise and the people of Hell will enter Hell. Then a caller will stand between the two and proclaim, 'O people of Hell, there is no death! O people of Paradise, there is no death! It is eternal.' The joy of the people of Paradise will increase and the despair of the people of Hell will increase." (Bukhāri)

In a narration of Muslim, it states that the Holy Prophet ﷺ said, "Death will be brought like a horned ram, and will be made to stand between Paradise and Hell. It will be said, 'O people of Paradise, do you know what this is?' They will raise their heads and say, 'Yes, this is death.'

Then the command will be given for death to be slaughtered. Then it will be said, 'O people of Paradise, it is eternal, there is no death! O people of Hell, it is eternal, there is no death!" Then the Holy Prophet ﷺ recited,

"And warn them of the Day of grief and regrets, while now they are in a state of carelessness and they believe not." (19:39)

The Holy Prophet ﷺ mentioned that everything besides man can hear the screams of the dead. If a man heard it, he would fall unconscious. The pious deceased person tells the people to hasten with his coffin, for if they saw where he was heading, they would hurry thereto themselves. The evil soul pleads with the people not to hurry, for if they saw where he was going, they would never take him there.

After burial, two dark, blue-eyed angels appear before the deceased. Salāh prevents them from approaching near the head side saying, "Do not approach from this direction because he used to engage in Salāh during the night for fear of the grave." Obedience to parents will shield him from the side of his feet, charity from the right side and fasting from the left.

Think for a Moment

This is but for a few days, where after, the everlasting journey to the Hereafter commences. There, a person will not be able to recite Subhān-Allāh or Alhamdulillāh even once. The life in this world is the only capital that a person has to invest for the Hereafter. If the capital is exhausted, a person cannot do any business. Time passes by constantly. When he decides to act it might be too late.

Angel Isrāfeel ﷺ is at present waiting with the trumpet in his mouth, waiting for Allāh's ﷻ command to blow it. Once he blows the trumpet, all of creation will be overcome with a strange anxiety. When he blows it for the second time, the universe will be annihilated, except for a few angels. Thereafter, Allāh ﷻ will ask the Angel of Death, "Who is still alive?" He will submit, "Jibreel, Meekāeel, Isrāfeel, the angels who carry the Arsh (Throne) and myself."

Allāh ﷻ will then command him to extract the souls of all these angels. When he will do so, Allāh ﷻ will again ask him who else still lives. He will reply, "Besides Yourself, it is only me." Allāh ﷻ will tell him, "All must perish besides Myself so you also die." Consequently, the Angel of Death will extract his own soul between Jannah and Jahannam. He shall give such an agonising cry at that time that if any of the creation existed then, they would all die in account of this cry.

He will then say, "If I realised the pain of death I would have been even more gentle when extracting the souls of the believers."

Only Allāh ﷻ shall live on. He will announce, **"Where are the kings? Where are the princes? Where have the tyrants gone? Where are their children? Where are those who ate from My provisions? To whom does sovereignty belong today? It all belongs to Allāh, The One, The Mighty."**

Thereafter, Allāh ﷻ will cause a continuous rain to fall from the skies, causing people to surface from their graves like sprouting plants. Thereafter, Isrāfeel عليه السلام will be raised, followed by Jibreel عليه السلام and Meekāeel عليه السلام. Then Isrāfeel عليه السلام will blow the trumpet for the third time and all of creation will be brought back to life. The first to be raised will be the Holy Prophet ﷺ. Everyone will be naked and will be gathered on a grand plain. Allāh ﷻ will not turn His attention to the people to pass judgement and they will weep so much that their tears will deplete and be replaced by blood. People will perspire so much that the perspiration of some of them will reach their mouths.

The people will then go to the Prophets عليهم السلام, pleading with them to beseech Allāh ﷻ to commence the reckoning. However, all will refuse except the Holy Prophet ﷺ. After his intercession on their behalf, Allāh ﷻ will begin the reckoning. All the angels will stand in rows and it will be announced, "Everyone's actions have been recorded in their books. Those whose actions were good should thank Allāh ﷻ and those whose actions were evil have only themselves to blame. All creation besides man and Jinn will have their revenge from each other, where after, they will perish forever."

No monetary recompense will work there. A wrongdoer will have to repay the claimant with his good actions. When their good actions have expired, they will be laden with the evil actions of the people who claim from them. In this manner, many people who initially had many good actions will end up bankrupt. The oppressor will then be doomed for Jahannam, while the oppressed person will enter Jannah.

The Day will be so severe that even the Prophets ﷺ, the high ranking angels and the martyrs will doubt their predicament. Questions will be asked about one's life, youth, knowledge and wealth. In search of a single action, people will approach their children, parents and loved ones, but will return empty handed.

Size of the People of Hell

When the people of Hell enter the Hell-Fire, they will be huge in their structure and size, in a form that none can comprehend except the One Who has created them. According to a Hadeeth narated by Sayyidunā Abū Hurairah ؓ, the Holy Prophet ﷺ said, "The distance between the shoulders of the disbelievers in Hell will be like three days travelling for a fast rider (on horse back)." (Muslim)

This increase of the disbeliever's body size will increase his suffering and torment. Imām Nawāwi ﷺ commenting on this Hadeeth said, "All of this is in order to intensify the suffering and all of this is possible for Allāh ﷻ. We must believe in it because the truthful Prophet ﷺ has informed us regarding it."

Imām Ibn Katheer ﷺ commenting on these Ahādeeth said, "So that their punishment and suffering may be more severe, as Allāh ﷻ says in the Holy Qur'ān,

لِيَذُوقُوا الْعَذَابَ

"They may taste the penalty." (4:56)

Food and Drink

Allāh ﷻ says,

لَيْسَ لَهُمْ طَعَامٌ إِلَّا مِنْ ضَرِيعٍ . لَا يُسْمِنُ وَلَا يُغْنِي مِنْ جُوعٍ

"No food will there be for them (people of Hell) but a bitter thorny plant, which will neither nourish nor satisfy hunger." (88:6-7)

The food of the people of Hell will be of no benefit whatsoever to them and they will not enjoy it in the least; this is one of the forms of punishments that they will suffer. Allāh ﷻ says,

إِنَّ شَجَرَتَ الزَّقُّومِ . طَعَامُ الْأَثِيمِ . كَالْمُهْلِ يَغْلِي فِي الْبُطُونِ . كَغَلْيِ الْحَمِيمِ .

"Verily the tree of Zaqqoom will be the food of the sinful, like the molten brass, it will boil in their stomachs like the boiling scalding water." (44:43-46)

The tree of Zaqqoom is described in another verse,

أَذَٰلِكَ خَيْرٌ نُزُلًا أَمْ شَجَرَةُ الزَّقُّومِ . إِنَّا جَعَلْنَاهَا فِتْنَةً لِلظَّالِمِينَ . إِنَّهَا شَجَرَةٌ تَخْرُجُ فِي أَصْلِ الْجَحِيمِ . طَلْعُهَا كَأَنَّهُ رُءُوسُ الشَّيَاطِينِ . فَإِنَّهُمْ لَآكِلُونَ مِنْهَا فَمَالِئُونَ مِنْهَا الْبُطُونَ . ثُمَّ إِنَّ لَهُمْ عَلَيْهَا لَشَوْبًا مِنْ حَمِيمٍ . ثُمَّ إِنَّ مَرْجِعَهُمْ لَإِلَى الْجَحِيمِ .

"Is that (Paradise) the better entertainment or the tree of Zaqqoom (cactus)? For We have truly made it (as) a trial for the wrongdoers. For it is a tree that springs out of the bottom of Hell-Fire. The shoots of its fruit-stalks are like the heads of devils. Truly, they will eat thereof and fill their bellies therewith. Then on top of that, they will be given to drink a mixture of boiling water. Then shall their return be to the blazing Fire of Hell." (37:62-68)

Furthermore He says,

ثُمَّ إِنَّكُمْ أَيُّهَا الضَّالُّونَ الْمُكَذِّبُونَ . لَآكِلُونَ مِنْ شَجَرٍ مِّنْ زَقُّومٍ . فَمَالِئُونَ مِنْهَا الْبُطُونَ . فَشَارِبُونَ عَلَيْهِ مِنَ الْحَمِيمِ . فَشَارِبُونَ شُرْبَ الْهِيمِ . هَٰذَا نُزُلُهُمْ يَوْمَ الدِّينِ .

'Then, you truly, O' you erring ones, the deniers (of Resurrection), will surely taste of the trees of Zaqqoom. Then you will fall in-

61

side therewith, and drink boiling water on top of it. Indeed, you will drink like thirsty camels! Such will be their entertainment on the Day of Resurrection." (56:51-56)

These verses explain the severity of this repulsive tree whose roots go deep into the bottom of Hell and whose branches stretch forth all over. Its fruits are so ugly that they are likened to the heads of devils, so that everyone may easily understand just how ugly they are, even though they have never seen them. Although this tree is so bitter and repulsive, the people of Hell will become so hungry that they will have no choice but to eat from it until they are full.

When they have filled their bellies, their food will start to churn like boiling oil, which will cause a great deal of suffering to them. At that point, they will rush to drink Al-Hameem, which is extremely hot water. They will drink it like camels that drink and drink but their thirst is never quenched because of some disease. Then it will tear their intestines and bowels. Allāh ﷻ says,

$$ وَسُقُوا مَآءً حَمِيمًا فَقَطَّعَ أَمْعَآءَهُمۡ $$

"They will be given to drink boiling water, so it cuts up their bowels (to pieces)."(47:15)

This is the hospitality that will be offered to them on that horrifying day. Furthermore, when the people of Hell eat this disgusting and vile food (Daree and Zaqqoom), they will choke because of its foulness. Allāh ﷻ says,

$$\text{إِنَّ لَدَيْنَا أَنكَالًا وَجَحِيمًا . وَطَعَامًا ذَا غُصَّةٍ وَعَذَابًا أَلِيمًا}$$

"Verily, with Us are fetters (to bind them) and a raging fire (to burn them), a food that chokes and a severe punishment."
(73:12-13)

The food that makes people choke is the food that sticks in the throat. Our beloved Prophet ﷺ explained for us the ugly and terrifying nature of Zaqqoom, "If one drop from Zaqqoom were to land on this world, the people of earth and all of their means of sustenance would be destroyed. So how would it be for the one who must eat it?" (Tirmizi)

Another kind of food that will be eaten by the people of Hell is 'Ghisleen'. Allāh ﷻ says,

$$\text{هَٰذَا فَلْيَذُوقُوهُ حَمِيمٌ وَغَسَّاقٌ . وَآخَرُ مِن شَكْلِهِ أَزْوَاجٌ}$$

"This, so taste it! This is the boiling water and puss and a multitude of other punishments of its kind " (38:57-58)

'Ghisleen' and 'Ghassāq' mean the same thing, which is the pus that oozes out of the skin of the people of Hell. It is suggested that it refers to the offensive discharge that flows from the private parts of adulterous women and the decaying skin and flesh of the disbelievers.

Four Types of Drink

When we ponder over the verses of the Holy Qur'ān, we will come to know that Allāh 🏵 has mentioned four kinds of drink that the people of Hell will have to drink.

Al-Hameem - This is an extremely hot water as Allāh 🏵 says,

يَطُوفُونَ بَيْنَهَا وَبَيْنَ حَمِيمٍ آنٍ

"They shall pass between it and the boiling water."

Al-Ghassāq - This is also one of the kinds of food and drink of the people of Hell mentioned earlier.

As-Sadeed (pus) - This is what flows from the flesh and skin of the disbelievers. Allāh 🏵 says,

وَيُسْقَىٰ مِنْ مَّآءٍ صَدِيدٍ . يَتَجَرَّعُهُ وَلَا يَكَادُ يُسِيغُهُ

"And he will be given pus to drink. He will drink it and it will not go down his throat." (14:16-17)

Imām Muslim 🏵 reports from Sayyidunā Jābir 🏵 that the Holy Prophet 🏵 said, "Anyone who drinks intoxicants will be made to drink the mud of Khabāl." They asked, "O' Messenger of Allāh 🏵, what is the mud of Khabāl?" He said, "The sweat of the people of Hell."

Al-Muhl - According to the Hadeeth of Sayyidunā Abū Saeed Al-

Khudree ؓ narrated by Ahmad and Tirmizi, that the Holy Prophet ﷺ said, "It is like boiling oil, and when it is brought near a person's face, the skin of the face falls off into it."

Allāh ﷻ says,

وَإِن يَسْتَغِيثُوا يُغَاثُوا بِمَاءٍ كَالْمُهْلِ يَشْوِي الْوُجُوهَ بِئْسَ الشَّرَابُ وَسَاءَتْ مُرْتَفَقًا

"And if they implore relief they will be granted water like melted brass that will scald their faces. How dreadful the drink! How uncomfortable a couch to recline on!" (18:29)

Clothing of the People of Hell

The people of Hell will be made to wear garments of fire as it says in the Holy Qur'ān,

هَذَانِ خَصْمَانِ اخْتَصَمُوا فِي رَبِّهِمْ فَالَّذِينَ كَفَرُوا قُطِّعَتْ لَهُمْ ثِيَابٌ مِّن نَّارٍ يُصَبُّ مِن فَوْقِ رُءُوسِهِمُ الْحَمِيمُ

"But for those who deny (their Lord) for them will be cut out a garment of fire, over their heads will be poured out boiling water." (22:19)

In another verse, Allāh ﷻ says, "

وَتَرَى الْمُجْرِمِينَ يَوْمَئِذٍ مُّقَرَّنِينَ فِي الْأَصْفَادِ . سَرَابِيلُهُم مِّن قَطِرَانٍ وَتَغْشَى وُجُوهَهُمُ النَّارُ

And you will see the sinners that Day bound together in fetters. Their garments will be of tar and fire will cover their faces." (14:49-50)

Sayyidunā Abū Mālik Al-Ash'ari ﷺ reports that the Holy Prophet ﷺ said, "A woman who mourns and wails over the dead, if she does not repent before she dies, she will be resurrected on the Day of Judgement wearing a shirt made from tar, a shield of covering."

Different Types of Punishment

In the Hell-Fire there will be various types of torment which will intensify the suffering of the dwellers of Hell. The intensity of the Fire is horrifying and traumatising such that a person will be prepared to give up everything that is dear to him in order to release himself from the punishment. However, this will never be possible. How eloquently Allāh ﷺ has stated in the Holy Qur'ān,

يَوَدُّ الْمُجْرِمُ لَوْ يَفْتَدِيْ مِنْ عَذَابٍ يَوْمِئِذٍ بِبَنِيْهِ . وَصَاحِبَتِهِ وَأَخِيْهِ . وَفَصِيْلَتِهِ الَّتِيْ
تُؤْوِيْهِ . وَمَنْ فِي الْأَرْضِ جَمِيْعًا ثُمَّ يُنْجِيْهِ

"On that Day, the sinful person's desire will be that he could redeem himself from the chastisement of the Hell-Fire by sacrificing his children, his wife, his brother, his relatives who sheltered him and all of that which is on the Earth so that it could release him (from Hell-Fire)." (70:11-14)

Sayyidunā Anas Ibn Mālik ﷺ relates that the Holy Prophet ﷺ said "One of the inmates of Hell who found the most pleasure in the life of this world will be brought forth on the Day of Judgement and will be dropped into the Fire of Hell. Then he will be asked, 'O son of Ādam, have you ever seen anything good? Have you ever enjoyed any pleasure?' He will say, 'No, by Allāh ﷻ, O Lord!'" (Muslim)

Just a short moment will make a disbeliever forget all the pleasure and good times they had enjoyed.

In another narration, Sayyidunā Anas Ibn Mālik ؓ mentions that the Holy Prophet ﷺ stated, "On the Day of Judgement, Allāh ﷻ will say to one whose punishment in the fire is the lightest, 'If you had whatever you wanted on earth, would you give it to save yourself?' He will say, 'Yes.'   Allāh ﷻ will say, 'I wanted less than that from you when you were still in the loins of Ādam, I asked you not to associate in worshipping besides Me, but you insisted in associating others in worship with Me.'" (Bukhāri, Muslim)

Hell has various levels; in some of them, the torment and horror is greater than others. The inmates of Hell will be given different levels of punishment according to their deeds.

Sayyidunā Samurah Ibn Jundub ؓ relates that the Holy Prophet ﷺ said concerning the people of Hell, "There are some whom the fire will reach up to their ankles, others up to their knees, others up to their waists and yet others up to their collarbones."

The lightest punishment has been mentioned in the books of Ahādeeth. In a Hadeeth of Bukhāri, the Holy Prophet ﷺ said, "The person who will have the least punishment among the people of Hell on the Day of Judgement will be placed on a hot ember and his brains will boil because of it."

Imām Muslim 🙵 reports from Abū Saeed Al-Khudri 🙵 that the Holy Prophet 🙵 said, "The person who will have the least punishment amongst the people of Hell will be made to wear shoes of fire, from which his brain will boil."   (Muslim)

Roasting of the Skin

The Fire of Hell will burn the skin of the people of Hell. The skin is a sensitive part of the body, where the pain is felt, for this reason Allāh 🙵 will replace the burnt skin with a new one, to be burnt again. This will be repeated endlessly.

Allāh 🙵 says,

$$ إِنَّ الَّذِينَ كَفَرُوا بِآيَاتِنَا سَوْفَ نُصْلِيهِمْ نَارًا كُلَّمَا نَضِجَتْ جُلُودُهُمْ بَدَّلْنَاهُمْ جُلُودًا غَيْرَهَا لِيَذُوقُوا الْعَذَابَ إِنَّ اللَّهَ كَانَ عَزِيزًا حَكِيمًا $$

"Those who reject Our Signs, We shall soon cast them into the Fire. As often as their skins are roasted through, We shall change them for fresh skins, that they may taste the penalty, for Allāh is Exalted in Power, All Wise." (4:56)

Melting

In the Hell-Fire, Al-Hameem (boiling hot water) will be poured over the heads. Due to its extreme heat, the internal organs of the person will melt. Allāh 🙵 says,

فَالَّذِينَ كَفَرُوا قُطِّعَتْ لَهُمْ ثِيَابٌ مِنْ نَارٍ يُصَبُّ مِنْ فَوْقِ رُءُوسِهِمُ الْحَمِيمُ . يُصْهَرُ
بِهِ مَا فِي بُطُونِهِمْ وَالْجُلُودُ

'As for those who disbelieve, garments of fire will be cut out for
them, boiling water will be poured down over their heads. With
it will melt and vanish away what is within their bellies, as well
as their skins." (22:19-20)

ayyidunā Abū Hurairah ﷺ said, Al-Hameem will be poured on
heir heads and will dissolve through until it reaches their sides
nd all their intestines will drop out, until it comes out of their feet,
nd when everything is melted, they will be restored as they were.

Scorching of the Face

he noblest, dignified and honourable portion of a person is his
ace, hence, our beloved Prophet ﷺ forbade us to strike the face.
)ne of the ways in which Allāh ﷺ will humiliate the people of Hell
s by gathering them on their faces, deaf dumb and blind on the
)ay of Judgement.

وَنَحْشُرُهُمْ يَوْمَ الْقِيَامَةِ عَلَى وُجُوهِهِمْ عُمْيًا وَبُكْمًا وَصُمًّا مَأْوَاهُمْ جَهَنَّمُ كُلَّمَا خَبَتْ
زِدْنَاهُمْ سَعِيرًا

"On the Day of Reckoning, We shall raise them (those gone
astray) on their faces (and they will be) blind, dumb and deaf.
Their abode shall be Jahannam. Each time it (the intensity of the
fire) lessens, We will increase its intensity (so that their
punishment should not be lessened)."(17:97)

69

لَوۡ يَعۡلَمُ الَّذِيۡنَ كَفَرُوۡۤا حِيۡنَ لَا يَكُفُّوۡنَ عَنۡ وُّجُوۡهِهِمُ النَّارَ وَلَا عَنۡ ظُهُوۡرِهِمۡ وَلَا هُمۡ يُنۡصَرُوۡنَ

"If only the disbelievers knew the time (in the Hereafter) when (while suffering in Jahannam), they will neither be able to ward off the fire from their faces, nor from their backs (because the fire will surround them) and they will not be helped." (21:39)

The Fire of Jahannam will scorch their faces and they shall be disfigured regarding which Allāh ﷻ says,

يَوۡمَ تُقَلَّبُ وُجُوۡهُهُمۡ فِى النَّارِ يَقُوۡلُوۡنَ يَا لَيۡتَنَاۤ أَطَعۡنَا اللهَ وَأَطَعۡنَا الرَّسُوۡلَا

"The Day when their faces will be overturned in the Fire as they say (in remorse), 'O! If only we had obeyed Allāh and obeyed the Messenger.'" (33:66)

The people of Hell will be dragged on their faces into Hell. Their pain at being dragged will be increased by the fact that they will be tied up in chains. Allāh ﷻ says,

فَسَوۡفَ يَعۡلَمُوۡنَ . إِذِ الۡأَغۡلَالُ فِى أَعۡنَاقِهِمۡ وَالسَّلَاسِلُ يُسۡحَبُوۡنَ . فِى الۡحَمِيۡمِ ثُمَّ فِى النَّارِ يُسۡجَرُوۡنَ

"They shall soon come to know (the error of their ways) on the Day of Judgement when yokes will be placed around their necks as well as chains. They will be dragged (like prisoners) into the boiling water after which they will be cast as fuel for the Fire."(40:70-72)

Blackened Faces

On that Day, some faces will be illuminated (bright with joy) while others shall be gloomy (depressed and scared) because of their disbelief and hypocrisy.

Allāh ﷻ says,

وَالَّذِينَ كَسَبُوا السَّيِّئَاتِ جَزَآءُ سَيِّئَةٍ بِمِثْلِهَا وَتَرْهَقُهُمْ ذِلَّةٌ مَّا لَهُم مِّنَ اللّٰهِ مِنْ عَاصِمٍ كَأَنَّمَا أُغْشِيَتْ وُجُوهُهُمْ قِطَعًا مِّنَ اللَّيْلِ مُظْلِمًا أُوْلَٰئِكَ أَصْحَابُ النَّارِ هُمْ فِيهَا خَالِدُونَ

"But those who earned evil acts, the punishment for evil will be similar to it and their faces will be covered in disgrace. No defender will they have from (the wrath of) Allāh. Their faces will be covered, as if it were with pieces from the darkness of night. They are companions (or dwellers) of the Fire, they will abide therein forever."(10:27)

The fire of Jahannam will surround the disbelievers on all sides like a bracelet or a bangle around a wrist, as Allāh ﷻ says,

لَهُم مِّن جَهَنَّمَ مِهَادٌ وَمِن فَوْقِهِمْ غَوَاشٍ

"There will be a bed of Hell (fire) and over them coverings (of Hell-Fire)." (7:41)

The 'bed' is what comes under them, and the 'coverings' are what comes over them. What is meant is that fire will surround them from above and below, as Allāh ﷻ says,

يَوْمَ يَغْشَاهُمُ الْعَذَابُ مِنْ فَوْقِهِمْ وَمِنْ تَحْتِ أَرْجُلِهِمْ وَيَقُولُ ذُوقُوا مَا كُنْتُمْ

تَعْمَلُونَ

"On the Day when the torment (Hell-Fire) shall cover them from above them and from underneath their feet."(29:55)

لَهُمْ مِّنْ فَوْقِهِمْ ظُلَلٌ مِّنَ النَّارِ وَمِنْ تَحْتِهِمْ ظُلَلٌ

"They shall have coverings of fire above them, and coverings (of fire) beneath them."(39:16)

The Fire of Jahannam will be so ferocious and deadly that it will leap over their hearts. It will penetrate through their bodies until it reaches their innermost depths.

Allāh ﷻ says,

سَأُصْلِيهِ سَقَرَ . وَمَا أَدْرَاكَ مَا سَقَرُ . لَا تُبْقِي وَلَا تَذَرُ . لَوَّاحَةٌ لِلْبَشَرِ

"I shall soon enter him into Jahannam. What shall inform you (what) Jahannam is? It neither spares nor leaves. It distorts the body." (74:26-29)

The scholars of Tafseer explain that **"It neither spares,"** means it eats bones, flesh and brains and it does not leave anything untouched. Allāh ﷻ says in another verse,

كَلَّا لَيُنْبَذَنَّ فِي الْحُطَمَةِ . وَمَا أَدْرَاكَ مَا الْحُطَمَةُ . نَارُ اللهِ الْمُوقَدَةُ . الَّتِي تَطَّلِعُ عَلَى

الْأَفْئِدَةِ

72

"By no means! He will be sure to be thrown into Hutamah (that which breaks into pieces). And what will explain to you what that which breaks into pieces is? It is the fire of the wrath of Allāh, kindled to a blaze; that which mounts right to the hearts." (104:4-7)

The horrifying situation will not cease here. Hadeeth narrated by Imām Bukhāri ﷺ and Imām Muslim ﷺ further elucidate the pitiful state of the dweller of Hell.

"A man will be brought forth on the Day of Judgement and thrown in the Fire. Then his intestines will be spilt out into the Fire, and he will be forced to walk around and around like a donkey in a treadmill. The people of Hell will gather around him and will say, "O' so and so, what is wrong with you? Did you not enjoin us to do good and forbid us to do evil?' He will say, 'I used to order you to do good, but I did not do it and I used to forbid from evil, but I used to do it myself.'" (Bukhāri, Muslim)

One of the people whose internal organs will be spilt out in Hell is Amr Ibn Lu'ay, who was the first to change the religion of the Arabs. The Holy Prophet ﷺ saw him dragging his own internal organs in Hell. Imām Muslim ﷺ reports from Sayyidunā Jābir Ibn Abdullāh ﷺ that the Holy Prophet ﷺ said, "I saw Amr Ibn Āmir Al -Khuzā'i dragging his own internal organs in Hell, and he was the one to institute As-Sā'ibah (a she-camel let loose for free pasture for the sake of idols, upon which no load was allowed to be carried)"

Chains, Fetters (Leg Cuffs) and Hammers of Hell

Allāh ﷻ has prepared different means to punish the people of Hell. A few verses of the Holy Qur'ān which explain this type of punishment are,

إِنَّا أَعْتَدْنَا لِلْكَافِرِينَ سَلَاسِلَ وَأَغْلَالًا وَسَعِيرًا

"For the rejecters, We have prepared iron chains, yokes and a blazing Fire." (76:4)

إِنَّ لَدَيْنَا أَنكَالًا وَجَحِيمًا . وَطَعَامًا ذَا غُصَّةٍ وَعَذَابًا أَلِيمًا

"With Us are fetters (to bind them) and a Fire (to burn them) and a food that chokes and a painful punishment." (73:12-13)

The yokes will be placed around their necks.

إِذِ الْأَغْلَالُ فِي أَعْنَاقِهِمْ وَالسَّلَاسِلُ يُسْحَبُونَ

"When yokes will be placed around their necks, as well as chains. They will be dragged." (40:71)

The chains are another kind of punishment with which the wrong-doers will be shackled, just as criminals are chained in this world. Read how the Holy Qur'ān describes them:

خُذُوهُ فَغُلُّوهُ . ثُمَّ الْجَحِيمَ صَلُّوهُ . ثُمَّ فِي سِلْسِلَةٍ ذَرْعُهَا سَبْعُونَ ذِرَاعًا فَاسْلُكُوهُ

"Seize him and bind him, then burn him in the blazing Fire, fur-

74

ther, make him march in a chain, which has a length of seventy cubits." (69:30-32)

Allāh ﷻ has assigned for the people of Hell hooked rods of iron, which are like hammers to beat the evildoers. When they try to escape from the Fire, they will be thrown even deeper into Hell.

$$وَلَهُمْ مَقَامِعُ مِنْ حَدِيدٍ . كُلَّمَا أَرَادُوا أَنْ يَخْرُجُوا مِنْهَا مِنْ غَمٍّ أُعِيدُوا فِيهَا وَذُوقُوا عَذَابَ الْحَرِيقِ$$

"And there will be iron hammers for them. Whenever they attempt to escape from the punishment out of grief, they will be returned and told, 'Taste the punishment of burning.'" (22:21-22)

Sorrow and Regret

We pray to Allāh ﷻ that He saves us from the Fire of Jahannam. Let us prepare for the inevitable death before it is too late when nothing will avail us from the regret and sorrow we will face.
In numerous verses, Allāh ﷻ portrays the sheer regret and sorrow of the people of Hell-Fire.

$$وَأَسَرُّوا النَّدَامَةَ لَمَّا رَأَوُا الْعَذَابَ وَقُضِيَ بَيْنَهُمْ بِالْقِسْطِ وَهُمْ لَا يُظْلَمُونَ$$

"They will hide their remorse when they see the punishment. Judgement will be passed between them with justice and they will not be oppressed." (10:54)

When a disbeliever looks at his book of records and realise his evils and sins, for which he deserves eternal Hell, he will pray for destruction and death. The disbelievers will continue their supplication and prayer for death when they are thrown into the Fire and its extreme heat touches them.

$$وَإِذَآ أُلْقُوا مِنْهَا مَكَانًا ضَيِّقًا مُّقَرَّنِينَ دَعَوْا هُنَالِكَ ثُبُورًا . لَا تَدْعُوا الْيَوْمَ ثُبُورًا وَاحِدًا وَادْعُوا ثُبُورًا كَثِيرًا$$

"And when they are cast into a constricted place therein, bound together, they will plead for destruction there and then! This Day plead not for a single destruction, plead for often repeated destruction." (25:13-14)

Their screams will grow louder and more desperate and they will call on their Lord, hoping that He will take them out of the Fire.

$$وَهُمْ يَصْطَرِخُونَ فِيهَا رَبَّنَا أَخْرِجْنَا نَعْمَلْ صَالِحًا غَيْرَ الَّذِي كُنَّا نَعْمَلُ$$

"Therein will they say aloud (for assistance), 'Our Lord, bring us out, we shall do righteousness, not the deeds we used to do.'" (35:37)

At that time, they will come to realize the error and foolishness of their Kufr.

$$وَقَالُوا لَوْ كُنَّا نَسْمَعُ أَوْ نَعْقِلُ مَا كُنَّا فِي أَصْحَابِ السَّعِيرِ . فَاعْتَرَفُوا بِذَنبِهِمْ فَسُحْقًا لِأَصْحَابِ السَّعِيرِ$$

"They will further say, 'Had we but listened or used our intelligence, we would not be among the companions of the blazing

Fire!' They will then confess their sins, but far will be (forgiveness) from the companions of the blazing Fire."(67:10-11)

Further in another verse Allāh ﷺ says,

قَالُوا رَبَّنَا أَمَتَّنَا اثْنَتَيْنِ وَأَحْيَيْتَنَا اثْنَتَيْنِ فَاعْتَرَفْنَا بِذُنُوبِنَا فَهَلْ إِلَى خُرُوجٍ مِنْ سَبِيلٍ

"They will say, 'O, Our Lord! (Whereas in the world we denied life after death, we now admit that) You gave us death twice (before our births and after living our lives) and granted us life twice (when we were born and now after death). We (also) admit our sins, so is there any way to escape (punishment)?'" (40:11)

It will then be made clear to them that the opportunity to ask for forgiveness has passed in the world and that they will have to remain in Jahannam forever. Hence, their prayer and begging will be turned down. Allāh ﷺ clearly paints the picture of the desperation of the people of Hell-Fire:

قَالُوا رَبَّنَا غَلَبَتْ عَلَيْنَا شِقْوَتُنَا وَكُنَّا قَوْمًا ضَالِّينَ . رَبَّنَا أَخْرِجْنَا مِنْهَا فَإِنْ عُدْنَا فَإِنَّا ظَالِمُونَ

"(In an attempt to save themselves) They will cry, 'O, Our Lord! (we admit that we were at fault) Our wretchedness (misfortune) over-powered us and we were a misguided nation. O, Our Lord! Remove us from here (and return us to the world). If we ever repeat ourselves (by doing what we did previously in the world), then we must surely be oppressors (sinful deserving of this punishment).'"(23:106-107)

Allāh ﷺ will say ,

$$قَالَ اخْسَئُوا فِيهَا وَلَا تُكَلِّمُونِ$$

"Remain disgraced (cursed) in it (in Jahannam) and do not speak to Me (about being delivered from it)." (23:108)

Allāh's ﷺ promise will come true and evident. They will reach a point where no scream or cry will benefit them and there will be no hope.

$$وَلَوْ تَرَى إِذِ الْمُجْرِمُونَ نَاكِسُو رُءُوسِهِمْ عِندَ رَبِّهِمْ رَبَّنَا أَبْصَرْنَا وَسَمِعْنَا فَارْجِعْنَا نَعْمَلْ صَالِحًا إِنَّا مُوقِنُونَ$$

"If only you could see the scene (in the hereafter) when the criminals (the disbelievers and sinners) will bow their heads before their Lord (saying), 'Our Lord! We have seen (resurrection and the Day of Judgement which we denied) and we have heard (everything that we refused to believe when your Prophets mentioned them to us). Return us (to the world) so that we may (accept Imān) and carry out good deeds. We are now certainly convinced (about everything that the Prophets and Messengers told us).'" (32:12)

This plea will be rejected because no one will be sent back to the world after death.

After that, losing all hope from Allāh ﷺ the people of Hell will call upon the keepers of the Fire, asking them to intercede so that Allāh ﷺ might reduce the torment for them. The people of Hell will also call out to the keeper of Jahannam, Mālik for help saying,

يَا مَالِكُ لِيَقْضِ عَلَيْنَا رَبُّكَ قَالَ إِنَّكُم مَّاكِثُونَ

"'O Mālik (the angel in charge of Hell)! Your Lord should settle
our matter (quickly, allow us to die instead of suffering here
eternally).' He (Mālik) will reply, 'You people will certainly have
to remain (here forever).'"(43:77)

In short, everything they will plead for will be declined and turned
down. There will be no coming out of the Hell-Fire, no reduction in
the punishment and torment and no respite. Rather, it will be an
on-going, perpetual, eternal punishment and at that time they will
be told.

اِصْلَوْهَا فَاصْبِرُوا أَوْ لَا تَصْبِرُوا سَوَاءٌ عَلَيْكُمْ إِنَّمَا تُجْزَوْنَ مَا كُنتُمْ تَعْمَلُونَ

"Enter into it! Whether you bear it with pleasure or you do not, it
will make no difference to you! (in any event, your suffering will
be the same) You are being punished only for what (disbelief
and sins) you used to do."(52:16)

Then their wailing will increase and they will weep for a long time.
They will weep until no tears will flow, then they will weep blood.
The tears will leave traces on their faces like heavy rain and floods
leave traces on the rocks and ground.

Prayer for Refuge from Hell

Imām Abū Dāwood ﷺ narrates in his Kitāb, Sunan Abū Dāwood that if anyone recites the following supplication,

$$ اَللّٰهُمَّ اَجِرْنِیْ مِنَ النَّارِ $$

(Allāhumma Ajirnee Minannār) "O' Allāh! Save me from the Fire," seven times after Fajr and Maghrib Salāh, if it so happens that he dies during the day, he will be secure from the Fire of Hell.

(Abū Dāwood)

Sayyidunā Anas ﷺ relates from the Holy Prophet ﷺ that he said, "No one asks Allāh ﷻ for Paradise three times, but Paradise will say, 'O Allāh ﷻ, admit him to Paradise!' And no Muslim man asks Allāh ﷻ for protection from Hell three times, but Hell will say, 'O, Allāh ﷻ, save him from me.'" (Mishkāt)

Imām Bukhāri ﷺ and Imām Muslim ﷺ report from Sayyidunā Abū Hurairah ﷺ that when the Holy Prophet ﷺ was discussing the angels who seek out gatherings of Dhikr, he said, "Allāh ﷻ asks them and He knows best, 'What are they seeking refuge from?' They will say, 'From the Fire.' Allāh ﷻ then asks, 'And have they seen it?' The angels will say, 'No, by Allāh ﷻ, O' Lord, they have not seen it!' Allāh ﷻ will further ask, 'How would it be if they had seen it?' They will reply, 'They would be even more afraid and anxious to escape from it.' Allāh ﷻ will announce to the angels, 'Bear witness that I have forgiven them.'" (Bukhāri, Muslim)

As we all know, Kufr (disbelief) and Shirk (polytheism) are those acts that will lead a person to eternal Hell. The way to be saved from Hell is through Imān (faith) and righteous deeds.

May Allāh ﷻ save us all from the torments of the Hell-Fire, Āmeen.

Paradise

In a Hadeeth Qudsi (sacred words of Allāh 🕌 narrated by the Ho
ly Prophet 🕌), Allāh 🕌 says, "I have prepared for my righteou
servants that which no eye has seen, no ear has heard and has nev
er crossed the mind of any human being." Then the Holy Prophe
🕌 said, "Recite if you wish,

فَلَا تَعْلَمُ نَفْسٌ مَّا أُخْفِيَ لَهُم مِّن قُرَّةِ أَعْيُنٍ جَزَاءً بِمَا كَانُوا يَعْمَلُونَ

"No person knows what is kept hidden for them of joy as a reward for what they used to do." (32:17)

Verse 46

وَلِمَنْ خَافَ مَقَامَ رَبِّهِ جَنَّتَانِ

"The one who fears standing in the presence of his Lord (on th
Day of Judgement) shall have two gardens (of Jannah)."

Verse 47

فَبِأَيِّ آلَاءِ رَبِّكُمَا تُكَذِّبَانِ

"So which favours of your Lord do the two of you deny?"

Verse 48

ذَوَاتَا أَفْنَانٍ

"Both these (gardens) shall be filled with branches (trees laden
with fruits)."

Verse 49

فَبِأَيِّ آلَاءِ رَبِّكُمَا تُكَذِّبَانِ

"So which favours of your Lord do the two of you deny?"

Verse 50

فِيهِمَا عَيْنَانِ تَجْرِيَانِ

"In both (gardens) there shall be two gushing springs (fountains)."

Verse 51

فَبِأَيِّ آلَاءِ رَبِّكُمَا تُكَذِّبَانِ

"So which favours of your Lord do the two of you deny?"

Verse 52

فِيهِمَا مِن كُلِّ فَاكِهَةٍ زَوْجَانِ

"In both these shall be a pair of every fruit (the same fruit with different flavours)."

Verse 53

فَبِأَيِّ آلَاءِ رَبِّكُمَا تُكَذِّبَانِ

"So which favours of your Lord do the two of you deny?"

Definition of Paradise

In the 3rd and final Ruku of Sūrah Ar-Rahmān, Allāh 🕮 mentions the blessings and favours that He has preserved for His rightful servants. He commences by proclaiming, **"The one who fears standing in the presence of his Lord shall have two gardens (of Jannah)."**

Jannah is the Arabic word to describe Paradise. In the dictionary, it is defined as, "a garden with dense trees." Jannah is an Arabic word which contains the letter Jeem and Noon. In Arabic, any word comprising of these two letters normally conveys the meaning of hidden or concealed identity. Jannah is that beautiful garden which is concealed and veiled from our eyes. We are told to believe in it.

Likewise, the Arabic word for the foetus is Janeen, which is also concealed from our eyes in the mother's womb. The word Junoon applies to the state of mental illness in a person which is again, hidden from our eyes. The word Junnah refers to a shield which conceals and hides a person from his enemy. Similarly, the word Jinn refers to the creation of Allāh 🕮 which is hidden from our naked eyes. Note that all these words contain the letters Jeem and Noon. This is just one glimpse of the beauty and eloquence of the Arabic language.

In the Islamic and religious terminology, Jannah refers to the eternal and spacious home which Allāh 🕮 has prepared for His true believers. A home beautifully decorated with unlimited favours, honours, blessings and bounties. May Allāh 🕮 make us from the occupants of this beautiful place, Āmeen!

Description of Paradise

The Companions ﷺ asked the Holy Prophet ﷺ about the buildings of Paradise. He replied with a wonderful description,

"Bricks of gold and silver and mortar of fragrant musk, pebbles of pearl and sapphire and soil of saffron. Whoever enters it is filled with joy and will never feel miserable. He will live there forever and will never die, his clothes will never wear out and his youth will never fade." (Ahmad, Tirmizi)

Allāh ﷺ says,

$$وَإِذَا رَأَيْتَ ثَمَّ رَأَيْتَ نَعِيمًا وَمُلْكًا كَبِيرًا$$

"And when you look there (in Paradise), you will see a delight (that cannot be imagined) and a great dominion." (76:20)

Gates of Paradise

Paradise has gates through which the believers will enter, with angels stationed,

$$جَنَّاتِ عَدْنٍ مُّفَتَّحَةً لَّهُمُ الْأَبْوَابُ$$

"Adn (where they will enjoy) eternal Jannah, with the doors opened for them (to welcome them)." (38:50)

In another verse Allāh ﷺ says,

85

وَالْمَلَائِكَةُ يَدْخُلُونَ عَلَيْهِمْ مِّن كُلِّ بَابٍ ۚ سَلَامٌ عَلَيْكُم بِمَا صَبَرْتُمْ ۚ فَنِعْمَ عُقْبَى الدَّارِ

"And (in addition they will be honoured when) the angels shall come to them from every door (of their palaces in Paradise)." The angels will say, 'Salām (peace) be to you for the patience that you exercised (in this world). How blissful is the outcome of the Ākhirah.'" (13:23-24)

Allāh ﷻ informs us that these gates will be opened when the believers reach them and they will be welcomed by the angels with greetings of peace.

وَسِيقَ الَّذِينَ اتَّقَوْا رَبَّهُمْ إِلَى الْجَنَّةِ زُمَرًا ۖ حَتَّىٰ إِذَا جَاءُوهَا وَفُتِحَتْ أَبْوَابُهَا وَقَالَ لَهُمْ خَزَنَتُهَا سَلَامٌ عَلَيْكُمْ طِبْتُمْ فَادْخُلُوهَا خَالِدِينَ

"Those who feared their Lord will be led to Paradise in groups. Until, when they arrive there, its gates will (already) be open (to welcome them before their arrival) and its keepers will say, 'Peace be on you! May you be pleased. Enter Paradise to live forever.'"(39:73)

It is narrated in a Hadeeth by Imām Bukhāri ﷻ and Imām Muslim ﷺ on the authority of Sayyidunā Abū Hurairah ﷺ that the Messenger of Allāh ﷺ said, "Whoever spends a pair (of anything) from his wealth for the sake of Allāh ﷻ, will be called from the gates of Paradise and Paradise has eight gates. Whoever will be from the people of Salāh will be called from the gate of Salāh. Whoever will be

86

from the people of Sadaqah will be called from the gate of Sadaqah. Whoever will be from the people of Jihād will be called from the gate of Jihād and whoever will be from the people of fasting will be called from the gate of fasting." (Bukhāri, Muslim)

In another Hadeeth, the Holy Prophet ﷺ said, "Whosoever spends a pair (of anything) for the sake of Allāh ﷻ will be called from the eight gates of Paradise." (Bukhāri)

Imām Muslim ﷺ reports from Sayyidunā Umar ؓ that the Holy Prophet ﷺ said, "Whosoever performs Wudhu and does it well, then lifts his gaze to the heavens and says: '**Ash hadu allā ila ha illallāh wahdahū lā shareeka lah, wa ashhadu anna Muhammadan abduhū wa rasūluh**, the eight gates of Paradise will be opened to him and he will enter it through any gate he wishes."

The Holy Prophet ﷺ described the width of the gates of Paradise, stating that the width between the two sides of the gate is like the distance between Makkah and Hajar or between Makkah and Basra.

The Holy Prophet ﷺ has informed us that the gates are opened during Ramadhān. Imām Bukhāri ﷺ and Imām Muslim ﷺ report from Sayyidunā Abū Hurairah ؓ that our beloved Prophet ﷺ said, "When the month of Ramadhān comes, the gates of Paradise are opened and the gates of Hell are closed."

Describing the magnificent distance between the two gate panels, there appears a Hadeeth in Musnad Ahmad which says, "The distance between the two gates-panels of one of the gates of Paradise is the distance of forty years walking, but a time will come when it would be crowded."

Coming back to verse 46 of Sūrah Ar-Rahmān, Allāh ﷻ says,

وَلِمَنْ خَافَ مَقَامَ رَبِّهِ جَنَّتَانِ

"The one who fears standing in the presence of his Lord shall have two gardens." (55:46)

In the beginning of the Sūrah, Allāh ﷻ mentioned the gardens of this world and in these concluding verses, He describes the gardens of the Hereafter. Although Jannah is itself an extremely large garden, there shall be many gardens within it, depending on the deeds of the people. This verse states that the person who abstains from sins and who is concerned about reckoning on the Day of Judgement, shall be blessed with two gardens of Jannah. Concern and worry for the reckoning on the Day of Judgement is a great contributing factor to motivate people to abstain from sins and to carry out good deeds. Allāh ﷻ states in Sūrah An-Nāzi'āt,

وَأَمَّا مَنْ خَافَ مَقَامَ رَبِّهِ وَنَهَى النَّفْسَ عَنِ الْهَوَى

فَإِنَّ الْجَنَّةَ هِيَ الْمَأْوَى

"As for the one who fears standing before his Lord and who restrains himself from carnal passions, then Jannah shall definitely be his abode."   (79:40-41)

Gardens of Paradise

Sayyidunā Abū Moosa Al-Ash'ari ﷺ once recited the verse,

وَلِمَنْ خَافَ مَقَامَ رَبِّهِ جَنَّتَانِ

"The one who fears standing in the presence of his Lord shall have two gardens." (55:46)

He then said, "There shall be two gardens of gold for the forerunners in Islām and two gardens of silver for those who followed them." (Hākim)

Allāh ﷻ further describes the two gardens by saying,

ذَوَاتَآ أَفْنَانٍ

"Both these (gardens) shall be filled with branches." (55:48)

There shall be an abundance of green and lush branches in these gardens, indicating that they will be filled with an abundance of fruits. Numerous verses describe the trees and fruits of Paradise. Allāh ﷻ has told us that there are grape vines, date palms and pomegranate trees in Paradise, as well as lote trees and many other types of trees in Paradise. In Sūrah An-Naba', He says,

إِنَّ لِلْمُتَّقِينَ مَفَازًا حَدَآئِقَ وَأَعْنَابًا

"Verily for the God-fearing, there will be success (Paradise) gardens and grape vines." (78:31-32)

89

In Sūrah Ar-Rahmān He further on says,

$$فِيهِمَا فَاكِهَةٌ وَنَخْلٌ وَرُمَّانٌ$$

"In them both will be fruits and date palms and pomegranates." (55:68)

In Sūrah Al-Wāqiyah, He says,

$$وَأَصْحَابُ الْيَمِينِ مَا أَصْحَابُ الْيَمِينِ فِي سِدْرٍ مَخْضُودٍ وَطَلْحٍ مَنْضُودٍ وَظِلٍّ مَمْدُودٍ$$
$$وَمَاءٍ مَسْكُوبٍ وَفَاكِهَةٍ كَثِيرَةٍ لَا مَقْطُوعَةٍ وَلَا مَمْنُوعَةٍ$$

"And those on the Right Hand, who will be those on the Right Hand? (They will be) among thornless lote trees and other trees laden (with fruits). (They will be enjoying all these bounties) in unlimited shade. (The environment will be without harsh sunshine and although they will have ample light, they will feel comfortable like a person who is shaded). And (enjoying the refreshing) flowing water and an abundance of fruits (of all types) that will not come to an end (because another fruit will immediately grow in the place of a plucked one) and will not be restricted (they will have as much as they please)." (56:27-33)

In other verses, He says,

$$مُتَّكِئِينَ فِيهَا يَدْعُونَ فِيهَا بِفَاكِهَةٍ كَثِيرَةٍ وَشَرَابٍ$$

"They will recline there, asking for (whatever they desire from) the abundance of fruits and drinks." (38:51)

وَفَاكِهَةٍ مِّمَّا يَتَخَيَّرُونَ

"And they will be served a variety of fruits to choose from."
(56:20)

Hāfiz Ibn Katheer ﷺ has efficiently described the greatness of the
fruits of Paradise by concluding that Allāh ﷻ conveyed about the
abundance and greatness of those fruits very briefly. He said, "The
lote tree (As-Sidr) does not bear any fruit other than some insignifi-
cant, inferior fruit and it is thorny just like the acacia tree (At-Talh)
which is used only for shade in this world (not for fruits). However
in Paradise, there will be many of them, growing beautifully and
bearing such abundant fruits that a single fruit will have seventy
kinds of taste and colour that resemble one another. So how do
you think the trees that are grown for their fruits on earth will be
in Paradise, like apple trees, date palms, grape vines and so on?
How do you think the flowers will be?"

In short, there will be what no eye has seen, no ear has heard and
no human heart can comprehend and we ask Allāh ﷻ to grant us
some of this, by His Grace, Āmeen!

The trees of Paradise bear fruits constantly unlike the trees of this
world, which bear fruits only on certain seasons. The trees of Paradise always bear fruits and offer shade. Allāh ﷻ says,

مَثَلُ الْجَنَّةِ الَّتِي وُعِدَ الْمُتَّقُونَ تَجْرِي مِن تَحْتِهَا الْأَنْهَارُ أُكُلُهَا دَآئِمٌ وَظِلُّهَا تِلْكَ
عُقْبَى الَّذِينَ اتَّقَوا

"The description of the Jannah that is promised for the pious (is that it has) rivers flowing beneath it while its fruits and shade will be permanent. This is the outcome (the position in the Hereafter) of those who adopt Taqwa."   (13:35)

The supply of fruits will be continuous and eternal and the people of Paradise will never be denied the access to these bounties. One of the delights that the people of Paradise will enjoy, is finding that its fruits are similar in appearance, but different in taste.

كُلَّمَا رُزِقُوا مِنْهَا مِنْ ثَمَرَةٍ رِّزْقًا قَالُوا هٰذَا الَّذِي رُزِقْنَا مِنْ قَبْلُ وَأُتُوا بِهِ مُتَشَابِهًا

"Every time they are given any fruit to eat there, they will say, 'This is what we were fed with before (in the world).' However, the fruits given to them shall only look the same (the taste, quality and other qualities will be very different from the fruits of this world).'" (2:25)

The second description states, **"In both (gardens) there shall be two gushing springs."** In addition to providing refreshing water, the springs shall provide a beautiful scene to watch.

In Paradise there are many springs that provide drinks of different tastes.

إِنَّ الْمُتَّقِينَ فِي جَنَّاتٍ وَعُيُونٍ

"Those who adopt Taqwa will definitely be (enjoying themselves) in Paradise and springs." (15:45)

Verily those with Taqwa shall be enjoying themselves under the shade of Allah's ﷻ throne on the Day of Judgement and thereafter, the shade of Jannah and springs. They will drink from a spring there (in Jannah) called Salsabeel (pure and clean water).

In Paradise there are special springs from which the Muqarraboon (close people) will drink, pure and undiluted, whilst the Abrār (righteous) will drink their water mixed with something else.

The first is the spring of Kāfoor (camphor) as Allāh ﷻ says,

$$\text{إِنَّ الْأَبْرَارَ يَشْرَبُونَ مِن كَأْسٍ كَانَ مِزَاجُهَا كَافُورًا عَيْنًا يَشْرَبُ بِهَا عِبَادُ اللهِ يُفَجِّرُونَهَا تَفْجِيرًا}$$

"Verily, the righteous (believers) shall certainly drink from a cup which contains (drink made from) a mixture of (water from the springs of Kāfoor which is) a spring (in Jannah) from which Allāh's bondsmen shall drink and which they shall cause to flow abundantly (whenever they wish)." (76:5-6)

Allah ﷻ tells us that the pious will drink from it mixed with something else, whilst the close servants of Allāh ﷻ will drink it pure and undiluted. The second spring is the spring of Tasneem, as Allāh ﷻ says,

$$\text{إِنَّ الْأَبْرَارَ لَفِي نَعِيمٍ . عَلَى الْأَرَائِكِ يَنظُرُونَ . تَعْرِفُ فِي وُجُوهِهِمْ نَضْرَةَ النَّعِيمِ . يُسْقَوْنَ مِن رَحِيقٍ مَّخْتُومٍ . خِتَامُهُ مِسْكٌ وَفِي ذَلِكَ فَلْيَتَنَافَسِ الْمُتَنَافِسُونَ . وَمِزَاجُهُ مِن تَسْنِيمٍ . عَيْنًا يَشْرَبُ بِهَا الْمُقَرَّبُونَ}$$

"Verily the righteous (believers) shall be enjoying bounties (comforts in Jannah) while looking on from couches (at the splendour around them). You will recognise the radiance of bounties on their faces (which will be bright and happy). They will be given pure sealed (preserved) wine to drink (completely unlike the impure and intoxicating wine of this world) the seal of which is musk. It is for this that competitors (those who strive) should compete (instead of competing for the inferior things of this world). Its mixture shall be Tasneem (which is) a spring (of Jannah) from which those close to Allāh drink." (83:22-28)

Another of the springs of Paradise is called Salsabeel, as Allāh ﷻ says,

وَيُسْقَوْنَ فِيهَا كَأْسًا كَانَ مِزَاجُهَا زَنْجَبِيلًا عَيْنًا فِيهَا تُسَمَّى سَلْسَبِيلًا

"They will be given to drink from cups containing a (wonderful) ginger mixture, (they will drink from) a spring there (in Jannah) called Salsabeel (pure and clean water)." (76:16-17)

Allāh ﷻ describes the third characteristic of these gardens when He says,

فِيهِمَا مِن كُلِّ فَاكِهَةٍ زَوْجَانِ

"In both there shall be a pair of every fruit." (55:52)

One type of fruits will be similar to what we see in this world while the other will be seen only in Jannah. Some commentator mention that one type of fruits will be fresh, while the other type will be dried. However, both will be equal in taste. Sayyidunā Abdullāh Ibn Abbās ؓ has mentioned that the "pair" refers to the sweet and sour fruits that are found in this world, which will be found in Jannah. However, bitter fruit like the wild gourd (bitter apple) shall be sweet in Jannah. (Roohul Ma'āni)

Verse 54

مُتَّكِئِيْنَ عَلٰى فُرُشٍ بَطَآئِنُهَا مِنْ إِسْتَبْرَقٍ وَجَنَى الْجَنَّتَيْنِ دَانٍ

"The people (of Jannah) shall recline on bedding lined with thick silk. The fruit of both gardens shall be near at hand."

Verse 55

فَبِأَيِّ آلَاءِ رَبِّكُمَا تُكَذِّبَانِ

"So which favours of your Lord do the two of you deny?"

Describing the bounties awaiting the righteous in Jannah, Allah ﷻ speaks about their beddings, **"The people (of Jannah) shall recline on bedding lined with thick silk."**

This verse tells us that the inner lining of this bedding will be made from thick silk. In this world, the outer lining of a bedding is usually decorated and made from material that is far more expensive than the material used for the inner lining. Sayyidunā Abdullāh Ibn Mas'ood ؓ states, "You have been told that the inner lining of the beddings of Jannah are made of thick silk. You can then imagine how beautiful and comfortable the outer linings are."

95

Saeed Ibn Jubair 🙵 said, "The inner lining is thick silk. If you want to know what the outer lining shall be made of, then read the verse of Sūrah Alif Lām Meem Sajdah where Allāh 🙶 says,

$$فَلَا تَعْلَمُ نَفْسٌ مَّآ أُخْفِيَ لَهُم مِّن قُرَّةِ أَعْيُنٍ جَزَآءً بِمَا كَانُوا يَعْمَلُونَ$$

"No soul knows what pleasures are hidden for him as a reward for the deeds he carries out." (32:17)

This means nothing can be said about the beauty of the outer lining. One will only know the reality of this in Jannah.

Allah 🙶 continues, **"The fruits of both gardens shall be near at hand."** Sayyidunā Abdullāh Ibn Abbās 🙵 mentioned that if Allāh's 🙶 friends in Jannah wish to pluck fruit while standing, they may do so. They may also pluck fruit while sitting or even lying down. In every condition, the fruit will be close by. (Roohul Ma'āni).

In another verse, Allāh 🙶 states,

$$وَدَانِيَةً عَلَيْهِمْ ظِلَالُهَا وَذُلِّلَتْ قُطُوفُهَا تَذْلِيلًا$$

"Its shade (the shade of the trees) will be close above them and its bunches of fruit will hang low (making them within easy reach)." (76:14)

96

Trees of Paradise

Our beloved Prophet ﷺ informed us of amazing accounts of some of the trees of Paradise which indicates that they are gigantic. By trying to imagine and comprehend them makes a person's head spin. In the Hadeeth of Bukhāri and Muslim, the Holy Prophet ﷺ says, "In Paradise there is a tree which the rider of a swift horse would need one hundred years to pass beneath."

In another Hadeeth of Bukhāri, Sayyidunā Abū Hurairah ﷺ narrates that the Holy Prophet ﷺ said, "In Paradise there is a tree in whose shade, a traveller could travel for a hundred years. Recite if you wish,

وَظِلٍّ مَّمْدُودٍ
"In long extended shade." (56:30)

Sayyidunā Abū Hurairah ﷺ and Sayyidunā Sahl Ibn Sa'd ﷺ both narrate that the Holy Prophet ﷺ said, "In Paradise there is a tree under whose shade a traveller could travel for one hundred years and not reach the edge of it."

Sidratul Muntahā
(The Lote Tree of Eternity)

Sayyidah Asmā Bint Abū Bakr ﷺ says that she heard from the Holy Prophet ﷺ about the Lote Tree of Eternity. He said, "A horse rider would travel within its branches for a hundred years or a rider would ride within its shadow for a hundred years. Within it are

97

butterflies of gold and fruits as big as large earthen jars." (Tirmizi)

The Lote Tree is located in the seventh heaven to the right of the Throne. It is called Muntahā because it is at the end of Paradise or because no one could go beyond it. Also, the knowledge of the angels ends here and what is beyond it, only Allāh ﷻ knows. Some say that the butterflies mentioned are actually angels whose wings shine as wings of butterflies.

The Wives of the People of Jannah

Verse 56

فِيْهِنَّ قَاصِرَاتُ الطَّرْفِ لَمْ يَطْمِثْهُنَّ إِنْسٌ قَبْلَهُمْ وَلَا جَانٌّ

"In these gardens, there shall be maidens with lowered gazes whom no man or Jinn has ever touched."

Verse 57

فَبِأَيِّ آلَاءِ رَبِّكُمَا تُكَذِّبَانِ

"So which favours of your Lord do the two of you deny?"

Verse 58

كَأَنَّهُنَّ الْيَاقُوتُ وَالْمَرْجَانُ

"They seem to appear like rubies and pearls."

Verse 59

فَبِأَيِّ آلَاءِ رَبِّكُمَا تُكَذِّبَانِ

"So which favours of your Lord do the two of you deny?"

Verse 60

هَلْ جَزَاءُ الْإِحْسَانِ إِلَّا الْإِحْسَانُ

"Can the reward of good be anything but good."

Verse 61

فَبِأَيِّ آلَاءِ رَبِّكُمَا تُكَذِّبَانِ

"So which favours of your Lord do the two of you deny?"

The men of Jannah shall have their worldly wives as well as wives from the 'Hoor-Ein'. These wives will be extremely beautiful and shall have eyes fixed for none other than their husbands. Allāh ﷻ refers to this when he says, **"In these gardens there shall be maidens with lowered gazes."** In addition to this, **"No man or Jinn has ever touched them."**

Describing their beauty, Allāh ﷻ says, **"They seem to appear like rubies and pearls."**

Wife of this World

Regarding a believer's wife of this world, Allāh ﷻ says,

جَنَّاتُ عَدْنٍ يَدْخُلُونَهَا وَمَنْ صَلَحَ مِنْ آبَائِهِمْ وَأَزْوَاجِهِمْ وَذُرِّيَّاتِهِمْ

99

"Eternal Paradise in which they will enter together with all those of their forefathers, spouses and progeny who are worthy." (13:23)

Hence, if a believer's wife is righteous and the believer enters Paradise, then his worldly wife would be his eternal life partner in Paradise too. In Sūrah Yāseen it states,

هُمْ وَأَزْوَاجُهُمْ فِي ظِلَالٍ عَلَى الْأَرَآئِكِ مُتَّكِئُونَ

"They and their wives will be in pleasant shade, reclining on thrones." (36:56)

In another verse it says,

أُدْخُلُوا الْجَنَّةَ أَنْتُمْ وَأَزْوَاجُكُمْ تُحْبَرُونَ

"Enter Paradise, you and your wives in happiness." (43:70)

A question is usually asked at this juncture, that if a woman married more than once due to her husband passing away or due to divorce from the first husband, then who will she be with, the first one or the last one? According to the different narrations, it seems that a woman will be with the last husband.

It is narrated in Tabarāni that Sayyidunā Mu'āwiya Ibn Abi Sufyān ﷺ proposed to Sayyidah Ummud-Dhardā ﷺ as to marry him, but she refused saying, "I heard Abū Dhardā ﷺ say that the Holy Prophet ﷺ said. 'A woman will be with the last of her husbands."

Ibn Asākir 🕮 reports that Sayyidah Asmā Bint Abi Bakr 🕮 was married to Sayyidunā Zubair Ibnul-Awwām 🕮 who was harsh towards her. She came to her father (Sayyidunā Abū Bakr 🕮) and complained to him. He said, "O my daughter, have patience, for if a woman has a righteous husband and he dies and she does not remarry after his death, they will be reunited in Paradise."

Imām Baihaqi 🕮 narrates that Sayyidunā Hudhaifah 🕮 said to his wife, "If you want to be my wife in Paradise, do not remarry after I die, for the woman in Paradise will be with the last of her husbands on earth."

This is one of the reasons why Allāh 🕮 forbade the wives of the Holy Prophet 🕮 to remarry after his death, because they will be his wives in the Hereafter.

In Tabarāni, there is a narration from Sayyidah Umme Salamah 🕮 that she asked the Holy Prophet 🕮, "O Rasūlullāh! Are the women of this world superior or the Hoors?" He replied, "The women of this world will have superiority over the Hoors just as the outer lining of the garment has superiority over the inner lining." Sayyidah Umme Salamah 🕮 then asked, "O Rasūlullāh what is the reason for this?" He answered, "Because they performed Salāh, fasted and worshipped Allāh 🕮. "

Allāh 🕮 will put light on their faces and silk on their bodies. The human women will be fair in complexion and will wear green clothing and yellow (gold) jewellery. The incense burners will be made of pearls and their combs will be of gold. They will say, 'We are the women who will stay forever and we will never die. We are the women who will always remain in comfort and we will never undergo difficulty. We are the women who will stay and we will never leave. Listen, we are happy women and we will never become sad. Glad tidings to those men for whom we are and who are for us." Hence, Allāh ﷻ will make the women of this world more beautiful and attractive than Hoors.

Allāh ﷻ will get the believers in Paradise married to beautiful and attractive women who were not their wives in this world. As Allāh ﷻ says,

$$ وَزَوَّجْنَاهُمْ بِحُورٍ عِينٍ $$

"We shall marry them to Hoors with wide lovely eyes." (44:54)

'Hoor' is the plural of 'Hoora' which means a woman who has eyes in which the white part is intensely white and the black part is intensely black. It also could mean that her beauty will be so striking that it will leave a person astonished and dumbfounded. 'Al-Ein' is the plural of 'Aynā'. The word Aynā is used for the woman whose eyes are big and wide and very attractive. This is considered a sign of beauty in a woman. In short, Hoor are those celestial women specially created for the people of Paradise, who are young, beautiful, fair skinned and striking in appearance, with intensely big dark eyes. Regarding the external and internal beauty Allāh ﷻ says,

وَلَهُمْ فِيهَا أَزْوَاجٌ مُّطَهَّرَةٌ وَهُمْ فِيهَا خَالِدُونَ

"And they will have pure wives in Jannah and they will stay there forever." (2:25)

Qatādah ﷺ mentions that these women will be pure from all external impurities such as menstruation, urine, excretion and saliva. They will also be free from all internal, evil qualities and habits such as malice, lying, hypocrisy, swearing and all other evil characteristics. Thus, they will not have within them the smallest amount of disobedience to their husbands.

Regarding their lovely shiny colour, Allāh ﷻ says,

وَحُورٌ عِينٌ . كَأَمْثَالِ اللُّؤْلُؤِ الْمَكْنُونِ

"And they will have fair females with big, lovely eyes who will be like hidden pearls." (56:22-23)

The women of Paradise will be like fresh pearls because of their cleanliness and fair skin colour. Allāh ﷻ states in another verse,

كَأَنَّهُنَّ بَيْضٌ مَّكْنُونٌ

"These women will be delicate and pure as if they were preserved eggs." (37:49)

Allāmah Āloosī ﷺ explains that this verse refers to those eggs which human hands have not yet touched, so they are clean from any dirt or dust. In the same way, the Hoors will be clean and free of all impurities. The comparison between the Hoors and eggs is also made because of the yellow-whitish colour of both, which is known to be the most beautiful skin-colour for women. Another explanation for this comparison is that the parts of an egg are known for being perfectly proportioned and conforming to one another. In the same way, all the body parts and features of the Hoors will go perfectly together. Allāh ﷻ says,

$$ كَأَنَّهُنَّ الْيَاقُوتُ وَالْمَرْجَانُ $$

"(In beauty) these women are like rubies and small pearls." (55:58)

The comparison between the Hoors and rubies is in transparency. A person can see through a ruby. In the same way, a person will be able to see through the Hoors because of the translucent nature of their skin and body. Allāh ﷻ has also compared the Hoors to small pearls because of their softness, whiteness and pleasant sight.

In the Hadeeth of Bukhāri, narrated by Sayyidunā Anas ﷺ, the Holy Prophet ﷺ said,

لَغَدْوَةٌ فِي سَبِيلِ اللهِ، أَوْ رَوْحَةٌ، خَيْرٌ مِنَ الدُّنْيَا وَمَا فِيهَا، وَلَقَابُ قَوْسِ أَحَدِكُمْ مِنَ الْجَنَّةِ، أَوْ مَوْضِعُ قِيدٍ يَعْنِي سَوْطِهِ خَيْرٌ مِنَ الدُّنْيَا وَمَا فِيهَا، وَلَوْ أَنَّ امْرَأَةً مِّنْ أَهْلِ الْجَنَّةِ اطَّلَعَتْ إِلَى أَهْلِ الْأَرْضِ لَأَضَاءَتْ مَا بَيْنَهُمَا، وَلَمَلَأَتْهُ رِيحًا، وَلَنَصِيفُهَا عَلَى رَأْسِهَا خَيْرٌ مِنَ الدُّنْيَا وَمَا فِيهَا

"One morning or evening in the path of Allāh ﷻ is better than the world and all that it contains. A hand span or a whip's length of

Jannah is better than the world and all that it contains. If one woman of Jannah were to glance towards the earth, she would fill the
space between the earth and the sky with light and perfume. The
scarf on her head is better than the world and all that it contains." (Bukhāri)

If just a small part of Jannah is better than the world and all that it
contains, then how will the rest of Jannah and all its pleasures be?
Also, if just the scarf on the head of one woman of Jannah is better
than the world and all of its contents, then how valuable is the
woman herself?

In a Hadeeth of Tabarāni, Sayyidunā Saeed Ibn Āmir ﷺ says that
that he heard the Holy Prophet ﷺ saying,

لَوْ أَنَّ امْرَأَةً مِّنْ نِّسَآءِ أَهْلِ الْجَنَّةِ أَشْرَفَتْ لَمَلَأَتِ الْأَرْضِ رِيْحَ مِسْكٍ، وَلَأَذْهَبَتْ ضَوْءَ
الشَّمْسِ وَالْقَمَرِ

"If a woman from Jannah were to look towards the world, she
would fill the earth with the fragrance of musk and her beauty
would overpower the light of the sun and moon." (Tabarāni)

In another Hadeeth of Tabarāni, the Holy Prophet ﷺ said,

لَوِ اطَّلَعَتِ امْرَأَةٌ مِّنْ نِسَآءِ أَهْلِ الْجَنَّةِ إِلَى الْأَرْضِ لَمَلَأَتْ مَا بَيْنَهُمَا رِيْحًا، وَلَتَاجُهَا عَلٰى
رَأْسِهَا خَيْرٌ مِنَ الدُّنْيَا وَمَا فِيْهَا

"If one woman from Jannah were to glance towards the earth, she would fill the entire atmosphere with perfume. The crown on her head is better than the world and all that it contains." (Tabarāni)

Sayyidunā Abū Hurairah ﷺ narrates that the Holy Prophet ﷺ said,

إِنَّ أَوَّلَ زُمْرَةٍ تَدْخُلُ الْجَنَّةَ عَلَى صُوْرَةِ الْقَمَرِ لَيْلَةَ الْبَدْرِ، وَالَّتِيْ تَلِيْهَا عَلَى أَضْوَإِكَوْكَبٍ دُرِّيٍّ فِي السَّمَآءِ، لِكُلِّ امْرِئٍ مِّنْهُمْ زَوْجَتَانِ اثْنَتَانِ، يُرَى مُخُّ سُوْقِهِمَا مِنْ وَّرَآءِ اللَّحْمِ، وَمَا فِي الْجَنَّةِ أَعْزَبُ

"The first group to enter Jannah will have the appearance of the full moon on the fourteenth night of the month. The next group will have the appearance of the brightest star in the sky. Every person from amongst them will have two wives and the marrow of their legs can be seen through their skin. There will be no unmarried person in Jannah." (Bukhāri, Muslim)

Outwardly, a person may consider it repulsive and disgusting to see bone marrow of the leg. However, this narration mentions that he will be able to see through her leg because of her beauty and not because of some defect in her. The purpose of mentioning this is to emphasise the transparency of their skin.

Other Gardens of Paradise

Verse 62

وَمِن دُونِهِمَا جَنَّتَانِ

"Other than these two gardens (of Jannah) are another two
gardens (reserved for all the other believers)."

Verse 63

فَبِأَىِّ آلَاءِ رَبِّكُمَا تُكَذِّبَانِ

"So which favours of your Lord do the two of you deny?"

Verse 64

مُدْهَامَّتَانِ

"Both (are) dark green."

Verse 65

فَبِأَىِّ آلَاءِ رَبِّكُمَا تُكَذِّبَانِ

"So which favours of your Lord do the two of you deny?"

Verse 66

فِيهِمَا عَيْنَانِ نَضَّاخَتَانِ

"Both have gushing fountains."

Verse 67

فَبِأَىِّ آلَاءِ رَبِّكُمَا تُكَذِّبَانِ

"So which favours of your Lord do the two of you deny?"

Verse 68

فِيهِمَا فَاكِهَةٌ وَنَخْلٌ وَرُمَّانٌ

"In both are fruits, date palms and pomegranates."

Verse 69

فَبِأَيِّ آلَاءِ رَبِّكُمَا تُكَذِّبَانِ

"So which favours of your Lord do the two of you deny?"

Verse 70

فِيهِنَّ خَيْرَاتٌ حِسَانٌ

"In them are good and beautiful women."

Verse 71

فَبِأَيِّ آلَاءِ رَبِّكُمَا تُكَذِّبَانِ

"So which favours of your Lord do the two of you deny?"

Verse 72

حُورٌ مَّقْصُورَاتٌ فِي الْخِيَامِ

"Fair damsels sheltered in tents (camps)."

Verse 73

فَبِأَيِّ آلَاءِ رَبِّكُمَا تُكَذِّبَانِ

"So which favours of your Lord do the two of you deny?"

Verse 74

لَمْ يَطْمِثْهُنَّ إِنْسٌ قَبْلَهُمْ وَلَا جَانٌّ

"Neither any man nor Jinn has ever touched them."

Verse 75

فَبِأَيِّ آلَاءِ رَبِّكُمَا تُكَذِّبَانِ

"So which favours of your Lord do the two of you deny?"

Verse 76

مُتَّكِئِينَ عَلَىٰ رَفْرَفٍ خُضْرٍ وَعَبْقَرِيٍّ حِسَانٍ

"The people of Jannah shall recline on green cushions and most beautiful carpets."

Verse 77

فَبِأَيِّ آلَاءِ رَبِّكُمَا تُكَذِّبَانِ

"So which favours of your Lord do the two of you deny?"

Verse 78

تَبَارَكَ اسْمُ رَبِّكَ ذِي الْجَلَالِ وَالْإِكْرَامِ

"Blessed is the name of your Lord, the Possessor of majesty and benevolence."

مُدْهَامَّتَانِ "Both (are) dark green!" (55:64). This is a one word verse and it means dark green foliage. The word is derived from إِدْهِمَامُ - Idhimām which signifies a meadow or garden to become dark green inclining to black due to excessive moisture or irrigation. This description is not assigned to the first two gardens. This does not in any way imply that they do not have this quality. The former gardens are described as ذَوَاتَا أَفْنَانٍ , having a lot of branches.

109

This includes the quality of dark green as well.

فِيْهِنَّ خَيْرَاتٌ حِسَانٌ, "In them are good and beautiful women." The word خَيْرَاتٌ - Khairāt, translated as good, refers to the good character of those women and the word حِسَانٌ - Hisān, translated as beautiful, refers to women who have beautiful features. These qualities will be common with the maidens of both the gardens, to which reference was made in the foregoing verse.

Market of Paradise

A human being has his own understanding of beauty which is restricted to his limited and deficient knowledge. Allāh ﷻ in His infinite knowledge and wisdom has described these women as beautiful, so we can imagine how beautiful these women must be.

Sayyidunā Anas ؓ narrates that the Holy Prophet ﷺ said,

إِنَّ فِي الْجَنَّةِ سُوْقًا يَأْتُوْنَهَا كُلَّ جُمُعَةٍ، وَتَهُبُّ رِيْحُ الشِّمَالِ فَتَحْثِيْ وُجُوْهَهُمْ وَثِيَابَهُمْ فَيَزْدَادُوْنَ حُسْنًا وَجَمَالًا فَيَرْجِعُوْنَ إِلَى أَهْلِيْهِمْ، وَقَدِ ازْدَادُوْا حُسْنًا وَجَمَالًا فَيَقُوْلُ لَهُمْ أَهْلُوْهُمْ : وَاللهِ لَقَدِ ازْدَدْتُمْ حُسْنًا وَجَمَالًا فَيَقُوْلُوْنَ : وَأَنْتُنَّ وَاللهِ ازْدَدْتُنَّ حُسْنًا وَجَمَالًا

"Definitely, the inhabitants of Jannah will visit a market every Friday. A northerly wind will blow and it will spread (goodness) upon their faces and clothes. This will cause them to increase in beauty. They will then return to their wives after becoming more beautiful than they were before. Their wives will say to them, 'We swear by Allāh ﷻ, you have definitely increased in beauty.' They will reply to their wives, 'We swear by Allāh ﷻ, you have also increased in beauty." (Muslim)

The beauty of the maidens of Jannah will be permanent and eternal and will never come to an end. Sayyidunā Abū Saeed ؆ and Sayyidunā Abū Hurairah ؆ narrate that the Holy Prophet ﷺ said, "When the people will enter Jannah, a caller will announce, 'Definitely for you is life; you will never become sick. For you is youth; you will never grow old. For you is luxury and comfort; you will never experience difficulty.'" (Muslim)

Age of the People of Paradise

In a Hadeeth of Baihaqi narrated by Sayyidunā Miqdād ؆ the Holy Prophet ﷺ said,

مَا مِنْ أَحَدٍ يَمُوْتُ سَقْطًا وَلَا هَرِمًا إِلَّا بُعِثَ ابْنَ ثَلَاثِيْنَ سَنَةً، فَإِنْ كَانَ مِنْ أَهْلِ الْجَنَّةِ كَانَ بِمِسْحَةِ آدَمَ وَصُوْرَةِ يُوسُفَ وَقَلْبِ أَيُّوبَ

"Every person who dies as a result of miscarriage or of old age or of middle age will be resurrected (around) the age of thirty. If he is from the people of Jannah, then he will have the height of Ādam ﷺ, the appearance of Yūsuf ﷺ and the heart of Ayyūb ﷺ."
(Tabarāni, Baihaqi)

The people of Jannah will never grow old and will remain permanently at the age of 33. The wisdom behind this age is that a person is at the height of his physical strength and his body parts are fully developed. Therefore, he/she can experience maximum pleasure from the bounties of Jannah.

Mansion of Paradise

Sayyidunā Abū Mūsā ﷺ narrates that the Holy Prophet ﷺ said,

إِنَّ لِلْمُؤْمِنِ فِي الْجَنَّةِ لَخَيْمَةً مِّنْ لُؤْلُؤَةٍ وَّاحِدَةٍ مُّجَوَّفَةٍ، طُوْلُهَا فِي السَّمَآءِ سِتُّوْنَ مِيْلًا،
لِلْمُؤْمِنِ فِيْهَا أَهْلُوْنَ، يَطُوْفُ عَلَيْهِمِ الْمُؤْمِنُ فَلَا يَرٰى بَعْضُهُمْ بَعْضًا

"Definitely in Jannah there will be a mansion made from hollow pearls whose height in the sky is 60 miles (111 kilometres). The believer will have wives in this mansion and he will go to them. These wives will not see each other." (Bukhārī, Muslim)

لَمْ يَطْمِثْهُنَّ - No human or Jinn has touched these women before. The reason for these women being virgins is because a person generally derives more pleasure with them. Allāh ﷺ will also change all the human women into virgins in Jannah.

These Hoors will be loving and equal in age. Under the commentary of the verse عُرُبًا أَتْرَابًا, "Loving in nature and equal in age," some scholars have translated the word عُرُب in two ways. One interpretation is that they have intense love for their husbands and the other interpretation is that they are experienced in love-making with their husbands.

مُتَّكِئِينَ عَلَى رَفْرَفٍ - The people of Jannah shall recline on green cushions and most beautiful carpets. Qāmūs explains that the word رَفْرَفٍ means silky fabric, greenish in colour which is used in making carpets, pillow cushions and other items of decoration. The noun عَبْقَرِيٍّ refers to every fine beautiful fabric or material and the adjective حِسَان Hisān (beautiful) qualifies it.

Sūrah Ar-Rahmān is repeated with verses that directs the attention to the blessings of Allāh ﷻ, his bounties and favours. The Sūrah concludes by informing mankind that even His Pure Name is Glorious and Majestic, so what can be said about His Being - the Most High?

How to attain Paradise

The Holy prophet ﷺ said,

مَا اسْتَجَارَ عَبْدٌ مِنَ النَّارِ سَبْعَ مَرَّاتٍ إِلَّا قَالَتِ النَّارُ: رَبِّ إِنَّ عَبْدَكَ فُلَانًا قَدِ اسْتَجَارَكَ مِنِّي فَأَجِرْهُ. وَلَا سَأَلَ عَبْدُ الْجَنَّةَ فِي يَوْمٍ سَبْعَ مَرَّاتٍ إِلَّا قَالَتِ الْجَنَّةُ: رَبِّ إِنَّ عَبْدَكَ فُلَانًا سَأَلَنِي فَأَدْخِلْهُ

"When a person seeks refuge from Hell seven times, Hell says to Allāh ﷻ, 'O my Lord, Your slave, so and so sought refuge from me, so give him refuge. When a person asks for Jannah seven times,

Jannah says to Allāh ﷻ, 'O My Lord, Your slave, so and so asked for me, so enter him into Jannah.'" (Abū Ya'la)

We should try to learn this simple and short Du'ā which has been attested and approved by the Holy Prophet ﷺ himself.

Secondly, we need to carry out good deeds constantly and continuously. Allāh ﷻ says, **"And for this, let all those strive who want to strive." (83:26)**

In another verse, He says,

$$\text{وَسَارِعُوا إِلَى مَغْفِرَةٍ مِّن رَّبِّكُمْ وَجَنَّةٍ عَرْضُهَا السَّمَاوَاتُ وَالْأَرْضُ أُعِدَّتْ لِلْمُتَّقِينَ}$$

"And hasten towards forgiveness from Your Lord and for a Jannah prepared for the pious, as wide as the heavens and the earth." (3:133)

We need to remember that the people of Paradise are the believers and monotheists. All those who commit Shirk (associating others with Allāh ﷻ), or disbelieve in Him or deny any of the principles of Faith, will not be allowed to enter Paradise. Their destination will be Hell-Fire.

The Holy Qur'ān frequently states that the people of Paradise are the believers who carry out righteous deeds. It states that it is the righteous deeds that will earn Paradise for the one who does them.

Allāh ﷻ says,

$$\text{وَمَن يَأْتِهِ مُؤْمِنًا قَدْ عَمِلَ الصَّالِحَاتِ فَأُولَٰئِكَ لَهُمُ الدَّرَجَاتُ الْعُلَى . جَنَّاتُ عَدْنٍ}$$

$$\text{تَجْرِيْ مِنْ تَحْتِهَا الْأَنْهَارُ خَالِدِيْنَ فِيْهَا وَذٰلِكَ جَزَاءُ مَنْ تَزَكّٰى}$$

"But whoever comes to Him (Allāh) as a believer and has done righteous deeds, for such are the high ranks (in the Hereafter), ʿAdn (Eden) Paradise, under which rivers flow, wherein they will abide forever; such is the reward of those who purify themselves." (20:75-76)

Thirdly, we need to control our desires in this world in order to achieve the high price of Jannah. Allāh ﷻ says,

$$\text{وَأَمَّا مَنْ خَافَ مَقَامَ رَبِّه وَنَهَى النَّفْسَ عَنِ الْهَوَى . فَإِنَّ الْجَنَّةَ هِيَ الْمَأْوٰى}$$

"And Jannah will be the place of residence for that person who fears standing in front of his Lord and refrains from evil desires." (79:40-41)

In a Hadeeth of Bukhāri, The Holy Prophet ﷺ said,

$$\text{مَنْ يَّضْمَنْ لِيْ مَا بَيْنَ لَحْيَيْهِ وَمَا بَيْنَ رِجْلَيْهِ أَضْمَنْ لَهُ الْجَنَّةَ}$$

"He who guarantees me that he will protect his tongue and private parts (by remaining chaste and protecting them from evil and only fulfilling his desires through lawful means), I will guarantee him Jannah." (Bukhāri)

Sayyidunā Anas Ibn Mālik ؓ narrates that the Holy Prophet ﷺ said, "Hell-Fire has been covered with desires and Jannah has been covered with difficulties." (Bukhāri, Muslim)

A person has to worship Allāh ﷻ regularly, five times a day, give Zakāt, observe the fasts of Ramadhān, eat only that which is law-

ful, stay away from temptations and sins and fulfil many other obligations. This requires a person to go against his desires and strive
to please Allāh ﷻ. On the other hand, it is very easy to fall into
sins. Hence, a person needs to refrain from the temporary tempta-
tion of this world in order to gain the eternal pleasure of the Hereafter.

In another narration, the Holy Prophet ﷺ said,

"When Allāh ﷻ created Jannah and Jahannam, He sent Sayyidunā
Jibreel ؑ to Jannah and said, 'See what I have prepared for its inhabitants.' Sayyidunā Jibreel ؑ came and saw what Allāh ﷻ prepared for the inhabitants of Jannah. He returned to Allāh ﷻ and
said, ' By the oath of Your honour, every person who hears about
Jannah will enter it.' Allāh ﷻ gave a command and Jannah was
surrounded by hardships and difficulties. Allāh ﷻ told Sayyidunā
Jibreel ؑ to go to Jannah once again and examine it. He returned
and saw that now Jannah was surrounded by difficulties. He returned to Allāh ﷻ and said, 'By the oath of Your honour, I fear that
no one will enter into Jannah now!'

Allāh ﷻ then said to him. "Go to Jahannam and see what I have
prepared for its inhabitants." Sayyidunā Jibreel ؑ came to Jahannam and saw what Allāh ﷻ had prepared for its inhabitants. He
saw that parts of Jahannam were riding on each other. He returned
to Allāh ﷻ and said, 'By the oath of Your honour, every person
who hears about Jahannam will avoid entering it.' Allāh ﷻ com-
manded and Jahannam was surrounded by desires. Sayyidunā Jibreel ؑ returned to Jahannam and said, 'By the oath of Your honour, I fear that everyone will enter into Jahannam.'" (Ahmad
Tirmizi)

Your Questions Answered

An outstanding book written by Shaykh Mufti Saiful Islām. A very comprehensive yet simple Fatāwa book and a source of guidance that reaches out to a wider audience i.e. the English speaking Muslims. The reader will benefit from the various answers to questions based on the Laws of Islām relating to the beliefs of Islām, knowledge, Sunnah, pillars of Islām, marriage, divorce and contemporary issues.

UK RRP: £7.50

Hadeeth for Beginners

A concise Hadeeth book with various Ahādeeth that relate to basic Ibādāh and moral etiquettes in Islām accessible to a wider readership. Each Hadeeth has been presented with the Arabic text, its translation and commentary to enlighten the reader, its meaning and application in day-to-day life.

UK RRP: £3.00

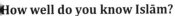

Du'a for Beginners

This book contains basic Du'ās which every Muslim should recite on a daily basis. Highly recommended to young children and adults studying at Islamic schools and Madrasahs so that one may cherish the beautiful treasure of supplications of our beloved Prophet 爲 in one's daily life, which will ultimately bring peace and happiness in both worlds, Inshā-Allāh.

UK RRP: £2.00

How well do you know Islām?

An exciting educational book which contains 300 multiple questions and answers to help you increase your knowledge on Islām! Ideal for the whole family, especially children and adult students to learn new knowledge in an enjoyable way and cherish the treasures of knowledge that you will acquire from this book. A very beneficial tool for educational syllabus.

UK RRP: £3.00

Treasures of the Holy Qur'an

This book entitled "Treasures of the Holy Qur'ān" has been compiled to create a stronger bond between the Holy Qur'ān and the readers. It mentions the different virtues of Sūrahs and verses from the Holy Qur'ān with the hope that the readers will increase their zeal and enthusiasm to recite and inculcate the teachings of the Holy Qur'ān into their daily lives.

UK RRP: £3.00

Other titles from JKN PUBLICATIONS

Marriage - A Complete Solution

Islām regards marriage as a great act of worship. This book has been designed to provide the fundamental teachings and guidelines of all what relates to the marital life in a simplified English language. It encapsulates in a nutshell all the marriage laws mentioned in many of the main reference books in order to facilitate their understanding and implementation.

UK RRP: £5.00

Pearls of Luqmān

This book is a comprehensive commentary of Sūrah Luqmān, written beautifully by Shaykh Mufti Saiful Islām. It offers the reader with an enquiring mind, Abūndance of advice, guidance, counselling and wisdom.

The reader will be enlightened by many wonderful topics and anecdotes mentioned in this book, which will create a greater understanding of the Holy Qur'ān and its wisdom. The book highlights some of the wise sayings and words of advice Luqmān ﷺ gave to his son.

UK RRP: £3.00

Arabic Grammar for Beginners

This book is a study of Arabic Grammar based on the subject of Nahw (Syntax) in a simplified English format. If a student studies this book thoroughly, he/she will develop a very good foundation in this field, Inshā-Allāh. Many books have been written on this subject in various languages such as Arabic, Persian and Urdu. However, in this day and age there is a growing demand for this subject to be available in English .

UK RRP: £3.00

A Gift to My Youngsters

This treasure filled book, is a collection of Islāmic stories, morals and anecdotes from the life of our beloved Prophet ﷺ, his Companions ؓ and the pious predecessors. The stories and anecdotes are based on moral and ethical values, which the reader will enjoy sharing with their peers, friends, families and loved ones.

"A Gift to My Youngsters" – is a wonderful gift presented to the readers personally, by the author himself, especially with the youngsters in mind. He has carefully selected stories and anecdotes containing beautiful morals, lessons and valuable knowledge and wisdom.

UK RRP: £5.00

Travel Companion

The beauty of this book is that it enables a person on any journey, small or distant or simply at home, to utilise their spare time to read and benefit from an exciting and vast collection of important and interesting Islamic topics and lessons. Written in simple and easy to read text, this book will immensely benefit both the newly interested person in Islām and the inquiring mind of a student expanding upon their existing knowledge. Inspiring reminders from the Holy Qur'ān and the blessed words of our beloved Prophet ﷺ beautifies each topic and will illuminate the heart of the reader.

UK RRP: £5.00

Pearls of Wisdom

Junaid Baghdādī ﷺ once said, "Allāh ﷻ strengthens through these Islamic stories the hearts of His friends, as proven from the Qur'anic verse,
"And all that We narrate unto you of the stories of the Messengers, so as to strengthen through it your heart." (11:120)
Mālik Ibn Dinār ﷺ stated that such stories are gifts from Paradise. He also emphasised to narrate these stories as much as possible as they are gems and it is possible that an individual might find a truly rare and invaluable gem among them.

UK RRP: £6.00

Inspirations

This book contains a compilation of selected speeches delivered by Shaykh Mufti Saiful Islām on a variety of topics such as the Holy Qur'ān, Nikāh and eating Halāl. Having previously been compiled in separate booklets, it was decided that the transcripts be gathered together in one book for the benefit of the reader. In addition to this, we have included in this book, further speeches which have not yet been printed.

UK RRP: £6.00

Gift to my Sisters

A thought provoking compilation of very interesting articles including real life stories of pious predecessors, imaginative illustrations, medical advices on intoxicants and rehabilitation and much more. All designed to influence and motivate mothers, sisters, wives and daughters towards an ideal Islamic lifestyle. A lifestyle referred to by our Creator, Allāh ﷻ in the Holy Qur'ān as the means to salvation and ultimate success.

UK RRP: £6.00

Gift to my Brothers

A thought provoking compilation of very interesting articles including real life stories of pious predecessors, imaginative illustrations, medical advices on intoxicants and rehabilitation and much more. All designed to influence and motivate fathers, brothers, husbands and sons towards an ideal Islamic lifestyle. A lifestyle referred to by our Creator, Allāh ﷻ in the Holy Qur'ān as the means to salvation and ultimate success.

UK RRP: £5.00

Heroes of Islām

"In the narratives there is certainly a lesson for people of intelligence (understanding)." (12:111)

A fine blend of Islamic personalities who have been recognised for leaving a lasting mark in the hearts and minds of people.

A distinguishing feature of this book is that the author has selected not only some of the most world and historically famous renowned scholars but also these lesser known and a few who have simply left behind a valuable piece of advice to their nearest and dearest.   **UK RRP: £5.00**

Ask a Mufti (3 volumes)

Muslims in every generation have confronted different kinds of challenges. In-spite of that, Islām produced such luminary Ulamā who confronted and re-sponded to the challenges of their time to guide the Ummah to the straight path. "Ask A Mufti" is a comprehensive three volume fatwa book, based on the Hanafi School, covering a wide range of topics related to every aspect of human life such as belief, ritual worship, life after death and contemporary legal topics related to purity, commercial transaction, marriage, divorce, food, cosmetic, laws pertaining to women, Islamic medical ethics and much more.

Should I Follow a Madhab?

Taqleed or following one of the four legal schools is not a new phenomenon. Historically, scholars of great calibre and luminaries, each one being a specialist in his own right, were known to have adhered to one of the four legal schools. It is only in the previous century that a minority group emerged advocating a se-vere ban on following one of the four major schools.

This book endeavours to address the topic of Taqleed and elucidates why it is necessary to do Taqleed in this day and age. It will also, by the Divine Will of Allāh ﷻ dispel some of the confusion surrounding this topic.   **UK RRP: £5.00**

Advice for the Students of Knowledge

Allāh ﷻ describes divine knowledge in the Holy Qur'ān as a 'Light'. Amongst the qualities of light are purity and guidance. The Holy Prophet ﷺ has clearly ex-plained this concept in many blessed Ahādeeth and has also taught us many supplications in which we ask for beneficial knowledge.

This book is a golden tool for every sincere student of knowledge wishing to mould his/her character and engrain those correct qualities in order to be wor-thy of receiving the great gift of Ilm from Allāh ﷻ.   **UK RRP: £3.00**

Stories for Children

"Stories for Children" - is a wonderful gift presented to the readers personally, the author himself, especially with the young children in mind. The stories are based on moral and ethical values, which the reader will enjoy sharing with the peers, friends, families and loved ones. The aim is to present to the children stories and incidents which contain moral lessons, in order to reform and correct the lives, according to the Holy Qur'ān and Sunnah.

UK RRP: £5.